Life of St. Peter
A Biography of the First Pope

By François De Ligny SJ

Edited by Frank Rega

DEDICATION

This book is dedicated to Lilly.

CONTENTS

Introduction

Life of St. Peter
A Biography of the First Pope

Originally titled:

The Teachings and Acts of St. Peter, the Prince of
Apostles and First Vicar of Christ on Earth
by
François De Ligny SJ 1709-1789

Enjoy this 18th century biography of St. Peter, which draws upon scripture as well as upon ancient writings, including texts from the early Church Fathers. It was originally written in Latin by a French Jesuit and a prolific author, Fr. François De Ligny (1709-1789). I discovered a copy of this work translated into English by a Mrs. J. Sadlier, in a musty volume of Catholic writings printed in 1892. Fr. De Ligny's life of St. Peter was written over a century prior to that date.

Here is an opportunity to review your scriptural knowledge of the first pope, and to take a journey through the early history of the Church. Learn the real reason for St. Peter's coming to Rome, and why he might have later been exiled from the city. Learn why the "Babylon" the saint mentions in his First Epistle refers to Rome. Learn who was the first writer who dared to deny that St. Peter was ever at that city.

The author painstakingly proves, through ancient histories and the Church Fathers of the early centuries, that St. Peter's residence in the Eternal City cannot be refuted. Doubts about his presence there first arose in the 14th century; and in spite of the proofs contained in Fr. De Ligny's thoroughly researched work, controversy about St. Peter's residence in Rome persists to this day in some quarters. To give just one example, see the Catholic Answers tract: http://www.catholic.com/tracts/was-peter-in-rome, "Was Peter in Rome," for a discussion of how and why some Fundamentalists and Protestants continue to assert that he was never in Rome. While establishing beyond any doubt that St. Peter was in fact in the city, Fr. De Ligny contends that the twenty-five years the saint reigned as its Bishop and the first pope, were not consecutive years of actual residence there.

Fr. De Ligny subscribes to the thesis that St. Paul never rebuked St. Peter to his face; rather, the "Cephas" referred to in Galatians 2:11 was not the pope put a completely different person. For a further discussion of this issue, please refer to Appendix I.

♦♦♦

Chapter I

The Call of St. Peter

St. Andrew and St. Peter – St. Peter the Chief of the Apostles – Great Draught of Fishes – The Apostles Receive the Holy Ghost – Ananias and Saphira.

St. Peter, the prince of the apostles, and first vicar of Christ on earth, was the son of Jonas, or John, of the tribe of Nephtali; he was born in Bethsaida, a city of Galilee, seventy-five miles distant from Jerusalem, situated on the Sea of Tiberias. His original name was Simon. Some authors have fixed the date of his birth three years before that of the Blessed Virgin, and seventeen years before the birth of Christ. He was the brother of St. Andrew, and according to Epiphanius was older than he.

Before his apostleship he was married, and dwelt with his wife and relations in Capernaum, pursuing the trade of a fisherman, and by this means endeavoring to support his family. His wife was the daughter of Aristobulus, the brother of Barnabas, and she is said by Clement Alexandrinus to have obtained the crown of martyrdom. He was brought to our Lord by St. Andrew, who tells him he had found the Messias, and brings him to him who is the Christ. When our Lord beholds him, he says: "Thou are Simon the son of Jonas; thou shalt be called Cephas, which is interpreted Peter." [John 1: 42.]

1

That the Cephas who was reprehended by St. Paul for the inconsistency of his conduct with respect to the Mosaic rites, was not St. Peter, is the opinion of the best writers. Eusebius quotes Clement Alexandrinus as maintaining that this Cephas was one of the seventy disciples. This opinion is followed by the most learned writers of antiquity, by St. Jerome, by St. Gregory the Great, by St. Anselm, and by many others. [Please see Appendix I below.]

Some have supposed that St. Andrew and St. Peter were amongst the disciples of St. John the Baptist, and were anxiously looking for the expectation of the promised Messias. St. Andrew having heard St. John the Baptist call our Lord "the Lamb of God; behold he who taketh away the sin of the world" [John 1: 29], was convinced of his being the Messias, and hastens to impart the intelligence to St. Peter. He was equally anxious with his brother to see the promised Messias, him of whom the law and the prophets had written so much, so that when he beholds him he believes in him, and stays with him during the remainder of the day. After this the two brothers leave our Lord, and return to their ordinary occupation as fishermen.

About the end of this year, the first of our Lord's ministrations, it would appear that the Saviour of the world saw St. Peter and St. Andrew washing their nets on the shores of the Sea of Tiberias; he enters into the ship which belonged to St. Peter, and desires him "to thrust out a little from the land, and sitting down, he taught the multitude out of the ship, and when he had ceased to speak, he said to Simon:

Launch out now into the deep, and let down your nets for a draught, and Simon answering said to him: Master we have labored all the night and have taken nothing; but at thy word I will let down the net; and when they had done this they enclosed a very great multitude of fishes, and their net was breaking, and they beckoned to their partners who were in the other ship that they should come and help them, and they came, and filled both the ships, so that they were almost sinking, which when Simon Peter saw, he fell down at Jesus' knees saying, Depart from me, for I am a sinful man, O Lord." [Luke 5: 4-8.]

◆◆◆

This humility of St. Peter procures for them greater graces, for "when they had brought their ships to land, leaving all things, they follow him." [Luke 5: 11.] And for this promptness in forsaking the things of the world, to become the disciples of Christ, St. Peter is told, when he asks our Lord what they shall have who have left all things and followed him: "Amen I say, to you, that you who have followed me in the regeneration, when the Son of Man shall sit on the seat of his majesty, you also shall sit on twelve seats, judging the twelve tribes of Israel. And every one that hath left house, or brethren, or sisters, or father, or mother, or wife, or children, or lands, for my name's sake, shall receive a hundred-fold, and shall possess life everlasting." [Matthew 19: 28-29.] Our Lord is said to have baptized St. Peter and his apostles; the seventy disciples are said to have been baptized by St. Peter and St. John.

Several of the fathers assert that after his apostleship St. Peter separated from his wife, and lived in a state of continence for the remainder of his days. St. John Chrysostom, speaking of him, calls him an illustrious model of chastity. [de Virgin, c. 82.]

From this period St. Peter and St. Andrew closely unite themselves to our Lord, and do not leave him during the entire period of his ministrations. Going from thence they proceed to Capernaum, and accompanied by St. James and St. John, they enter their own house. There, too, our Lord enters, and heals Simon's wife's mother, who is sick of a fever: "They tell him of her, and he came and lifted her up, taking her by the hand, and immediately the fever left her, and she ministered unto him. [Mark 1: 31.]

Our Lord generally addressed his conversation to St. Peter, who usually answered on behalf of all the apostles. Our Lord had hitherto distinguished him from the other apostles by the tokens of dignity and honor which he had shown him. About a year before the events connected with his Passion took place, our Lord resolves to entrust to his keeping the Church which he was to found on earth. After having received testimony of his faith and of his charity, and of his zeal for the salvation of souls, our Lord says to him: "Thou are Peter, and upon this rock I will build my church, and the gates of hell shall not prevail against it; and I will give to thee the keys of the kingdom of heaven, and whatsoever thou shalt bind upon earth it shall be bound also in heaven, and whatsoever thou shalt loose upon earth it shall be loosed also in heaven." [Matthew 16: 18-19.]

St. Peter is often represented with one key in his hand, as a symbol of the one holy Catholic and apostolic church, and as an evidence of the primacy of this being granted to him, that thus there might be one fold and one pastor. By the three keys with which St. Peter is also represented as holding in his hand, it is shown that authority in heaven, in hell, and on earth, is granted to him.

On another occasion our Lord declares the infallibility of St. Peter, and his office of confirming his brethren in the faith; for at the Last Supper he addresses him thus: "And thou being once converted, confirm thy brethren;" or, as the most celebrated commentators seem inclined to render the passage, giving its proper force to the adverb, "thou in thy turn confirm thy brethren." [Luke 22: 32.] By the tribute which our Lord paid for himself and St. Peter, he desired to confirm the supremacy which he and his successors were to exercise over the Church. To St. Peter our Lord had consigned the mystical keys of the kingdom of heaven; and by this he and the Roman pontiffs were constituted his vicars on earth. In the Transfiguration our Lord made him also partaker of his glory, with two other apostles, St. James and St. John.

◆◆◆

On two separate occasions St. Peter shows his zeal and love for our Lord by casting himself into the sea, and not waiting until the ship would arrive at land.

When St. Peter heard our Lord predict his death and sufferings in Jerusalem, he expresses in the strongest language his attachment and devotion to him, and tells him he is ready to go with him to prison and to death.

Before the Last Supper, our Lord, having loved his apostles, loved them to the end; and he rises from the table, and takes a towel to gird himself with it, having first laid aside his garments; he then pours water into a basin, and begins to wash the feet of his disciples, and to wipe them with the towel wherewith he was girded. "He cometh therefore to Simon Peter, and Peter saith to him: Lord, dost thou wash my feet? Jesus answered and said to him: What I do thou knowest not now, but thou shalt know hereafter. Peter said to him: Thou shalt never wash my feet." He only permits his Lord to do so, when he tells him that "If I wash thee not, thou shalt have no part with me." [John 13: 6-8.]

He then has the privilege of following him to the Garden of Gethsemane, where, with St. James and St. John he is a witness of our Lord's being carried away as a prisoner, by Judas and by the crowd who accompanied him. St. Peter accompanied our Lord, and his heart is filled with zeal when he beholds him thus taken prisoner, and he stretches forth his hand and draws out his sword, and strikes the servant of the high-priest, and cuts off his ear. Our Lord turns round to St. Peter, and having healed the wound which he had inflicted on the servant, whose name was Malchus, he addressed him in the following words: "Put up thy sword again into its place, for all that take the sword shall perish with the sword." [Matthew 26: 52.]

When our Lord was brought before his judges, St. Peter accompanies him, and enters with him into the house of Caiaphas, where two of the servant-maids say to him that he was with Jesus of Galilee; this St. Peter denies before them all, saying: "I know not what thou sayest;" the second time he denies with an oath, saying: "I know not the man." And after a little while, those that stood by say to St. Peter: "Surely thou also art one of them, for even thy speech doth discover thee." Then he begins to curse and to swear, that he knew not the man; "and immediately the cock crew; and Peter remembered the words of Jesus which he had said: Before the cock crow thou wilt deny me thrice; and going forth, he wept bitterly." [Matthew 26: 69-75.]

So deep was the contrition of St. Peter for his denying his Lord, and so bitter were the tears which he shed, that they are said to have formed two furrows in his cheeks, which remained there during his life-time; and the life which he led from that time forward was of so mortified a nature, that he usually ate nothing but herbs or roots.

After his resurrection our Lord appears to St. Mary Magdalen, and bids her to go and tell his apostles and St. Peter, that he went before them into Galilee. Thus, by especially mentioning his name, he desires to show them that he has accepted the penance which Peter had performed for denying him.

After this our Lord shows himself again to the disciples at the Sea of Tiberias. Simon Peter and other disciples had gone fishing during the night but caught nothing; when the morning came they beheld Jesus standing on the shore, and they knew him not. He asked them if they have any meat. In reply to our Lord they answer him no, and he bids them cast their nets on the right side of the ship and they should find. In obedience to our Lord's directions, they cast on the side of the ship he directed them, and they are not able to draw for the multitude of fishes. The disciple whom the Lord loved, St. John, says to St. Peter, "It is the Lord." [John 21: 7.] As soon as Simon Peter hears this, he girds his coat about him, and casts himself into the sea. The other disciples come to the land in the ship with the fishes; and they find hot coals lying, and a fish laid thereon, and bread. Our Lord tells them to bring him some of the fishes which they had caught. St. Peter draws the net to land, full of great fishes, and the net was not broken. Our Lord then tells them to come and dine; they know it is the Lord. When they sit down Jesus comes and takes bread and gives it to them, together with the fish to eat. When the dinner is finished, he addresses himself to St. Peter and says:

"Simon son of John, lovest thou me more than these? He saith to him, Yea Lord, thou knowest that I love thee; and he saith to him Feed my lambs. He saith to him again, Simon son of John, lovest thou me? He saith to him, Yea, Lord, thou knowest that I love thee. He saith to him, Feed my lambs. He saith to him the third time, Simon son of John, lovest thou me? Peter was grieved because he had said to him the third time, lovest thou me? And he said to him, Lord, thou knowest all things: thou knowest that I love thee. He saith to him, Feed my sheep." [John 21: 15-17].

8

Our Lord by this declaration constitutes St. Peter and his successors the vicars and pastors of his Church, and then imparts to St. Peter even more joyful intelligence than this; for he tells him that the death of the martyr was to be his privilege: "Amen amen, I say to thee: when thou wast younger, thou didst gird thyself, and didst walk where thou wouldst; but when thou shalt be old, thou shalt stretch forth thy hands, and another shall gird thee, and lead thee whither thou wouldst not." [John 21: 18.]

After the Ascension of our Lord, the apostles returned to Jerusalem, and, assembled there, they proceed to the election of a successor to Judas. There St. Peter exercises his first act of jurisdiction, by presiding at the council that was held when Matthias was elected an apostle. [Acts 1: 15-26.]

Some time after this St. Peter consecrates St. James Bishop of Jerusalem; and in the year 34 celebrates another council, in the upper room.

On the day of Pentecost the apostles receive, in the upper room where our Lord had instituted the sacrifice of the Mass, the Holy Ghost. On that day, the Jews had accused the apostles of being full of new wine. St. Peter refutes their calumnies, and shows it was only a fulfillment of the predictions of the prophets; and so powerful is the sermon he preaches on the Resurrection and Ascension of our Lord, that three thousand persons are converted and baptized.

A few days after this St. Peter and St. John go up to the temple, where they meet, at the gate of the temple which is called Beautiful, a man who was lame from his mother's womb, and who was laid every day in the temple. He asks St. Peter and St. John for alms. St. Peter tells him that he has no silver or gold to give him, but bids him, "in the name of Jesus of Nazareth arise and walk." [Acts 3: 6.] The people, astonished at beholding the wonderful miracle, assemble in Solomon's porch, where St. Peter addresses them with such wonderful effect, that five thousand persons were converted. With his shadow many extraordinary cures are performed, and in the name of Jesus of Nazareth he performed many miracles.

The Holy Ghost had wrought a great change in him, for to his courage and boldness are united humility, gentleness and patience; always ready to yield to others, he humbles himself to every one. Ever desirous of being the servant of all, he never seems to exercise the authority with which he is invested unless when the duty of God requires it.

The Jewish priests and the Sadducees, jealous of the conversions which St. Peter had effected, and of the miracles which he wrought, cause him to be imprisoned along with St. John. On the next day they are brought before the princes, the ancients, and the scribes, who are assembled in council, together with the high-priest Annas and his kinsmen. There St. Peter declares to them "that it is by the name of Jesus of Nazareth that this man standeth before them whole." [Acts 4: 10.] As the assembled Sanhedrin could not deny the miracle, they address St. Peter and St. John, and charge them not to speak nor teach in the name of Jesus. This the apostles refuse to do, and say to them: "If it be just in the sight of God, to hear you rather than God, judge ye.

For we cannot but speak the things which we have seen and heard." [Acts 4: 19-20.] The apostles were then set at liberty.

Those who had become Christians had their attention fixed on the great blessings which they enjoyed on becoming members of the Church. Worldly riches and honors had no value in their sight; therefore the wealthy amongst them sold their possessions, and laid the money for which they sold them at the apostles' feet – who would make an equal distribution of the different sums thus presented to them, amongst the members of the Church who were in need of it. Among the different persons who sold their property, there was a certain man named Ananias, and Saphira his wife; they sold their field for a certain price (and by fraud, kept back part of it), and laid it down at the apostles' feet – the wife being conscious of this. Peter, as the chief of the apostles, deemed it to be his duty to check this fraudulent mode of acting, in the infancy of the Church, and he asks Ananias why Satan had tempted his heart, that he should lie to the Holy Ghost, and keep back, through fraud, part of the price of the field, and he shows him the nature of the fraud he had committed: "Whilst it remained, was it not thine own? And being sold was it not in thy power? Why hast thou conceived this thing in thy heart? Thou hast not lied to men but to God." [Acts 5: 3-4.] As soon as Ananias had heard these words, he fell down and gave up the ghost.

The young men who were present remove his body, and take it out and bury it. About three hours after this event had taken place, his wife, not knowing what had happened, came in, and St. Peter asks her whether she had sold the field for so much; and she says, in reply, that she had sold it for this sum. St. Peter says, in reply to her: "Why have you agreed together to tempt the spirit of the Lord? Behold, the feet of those who have buried thy husband are at the door, and they shall carry thee out." [Acts 5: 9.] And she immediately fell down dead before his feet; and the young men who had carried her husband to the grave perform the same office for her, and bury her beside her husband. This circumstance produced a good effect [a great fear] upon the whole Church, and upon all that heard of these things.

◆◆◆

Chapter II

Growth of the Church

The Apostles brought before the Council – Prudent counsel of Gamaliel – St. Peter at Joppe – He meets with Cornelius.

The apostles had given proofs of their divine mission by working a great number of miracles. These circumstances excited the indignation of the high-priest and of the other members of the Sanhedrin, especially as many sick persons had been healed by the mere shadow of St. Peter passing over them; and persons afflicted with diseases were brought from the neighboring cities, and were cured of their diseases by the miraculous powers which the apostles exercised. Such as were troubled with unclean spirits were also healed. The high-priest and the Sadducees resolved to put an end to this, and they therefore laid hands on the apostles, and put them in the common prison. But the angel of the Lord by night opened the doors of the prison, and leading them out bid them go to the temple, and preach there "all the words of this life." [Acts 5: 20.]

The officers in the morning are much astonished, at finding the prison shut but no man within. Whilst the chief priest and those assembled with him are in doubt as to what had become of them, a certain man comes and tells them that the men whom they put in prison are teaching the people in the temple.

The magistrates, when they heard this, go and bring them without violence – for they fear the people, lest they should be stoned. When the apostles are brought before the council, and the high-priest reminds them of the charge that had already been given them that they should not teach in the name of Jesus, and how they had disobeyed this command, and had filled Jerusalem with their doctrine, and would bring the blood of "this man" (for so the high-priest calls our Lord) upon them – to this St. Peter, in the name of the apostles, replies, "that we ought to obey God rather than man;" and he then openly charges the high-priest and those assembled with him, as having put to death Jesus, whom God had now raised up, and exalted with his right hand to give penitence to Israel and remission of sins; and he further adds, that he and the other apostles are witnesses of these things, and "the Holy Ghost, whom God had given to all who obey him." [Acts 5: 29, 31-32.]

The high-priest and the assembly, when they had heard these things, were cut to the heart, and but for the prudent counsel of Gamaliel, would have put them to death – who told them that, if it be the design or work of men, the preaching of the apostles will fall to nothing; but that it be of God, they could not destroy it. The council hearken to the words of Gamaliel, and scourge the apostles, and charge them not to speak in the name of Jesus, and after this dismiss them. The apostles leave them, rejoicing that they were deemed worthy to suffer reproach for the name of their Lord and Master; and they continue their preaching and teaching from house to house.

The number of those who joined the Church increased from day to day, and a great number of the priests embrace the faith. This wondrous triumph of the Church, and the progress which religion is making, stir up the hatred and enmity of its opponents against the faithful, and a great persecution is raised against the Church. St. Stephen is stoned and put to death, and all the faithful, except the apostles, are dispersed through the countries of Judea and Samaria. In the latter, Philip, one of the seven deacons, had converted many by his preaching and had performed many miracles. St. Peter and St. John go down to Samaria to strengthen the faith of the converts, by administering to them the sacrament of Confirmation.

♦♦♦

Amongst those whom Philip had converted was a person named Simon Magus. He had been a magician, and had seduced the people of Samaria, giving himself out to be some great person. When he saw the number of men and women that had been baptized by Philip, he also believes and is baptized. When he beholds that by the laying on of the hands of the apostles the Holy Ghost is given, he offers to give money to St. Peter if he should confer the same power on him, and enable him to impart the Holy Ghost on whomsoever he would lay his hands. St. Peter replies to his request in the following words: "May thy money perish with thee, because thou hast esteemed the gift of God to be purchased with money. Thou hast no part nor lot in this matter, for thy heart is not right in the sight of God. Do penance, therefore, for this thy wickedness, and pray to God, that perhaps this thought of thy heart may be forgiven thee, for I see thou art in the gall of bitterness and in the bonds of iniquity." [Acts 8: 20-23.]

Peace is once more restored to the Church, throughout Judea, Galilee, and Samaria. St. Peter, in the course of his missionary labors, and the apostolical superintendence which, as prince of the apostles, he bestowed on the Church, visits Lydda, where he finds a certain man name Eneas, lying on his bed for eight years, who was ill of the palsy. St. Peter says to him: "Eneas, the Lord Jesus healeth thee: arise and make thy bed; and immediately he arose." [Acts 9: 34.] The apostle also visits Joppe, where a certain disciple named Tabitha, who was full of good works and alms-deeds, becomes sick and dies. When they had laid her out in an upper chamber, the disciples sent to Lydda for St. Peter, who, when he was arrived, is brought by the faithful into the upper chamber where the good woman was laid out. There St. Peter finds assembled all the widows weeping, who show him the garments which Dorcas (for so the good woman was called) had made for them. St. Peter, having put them all out, kneels down and prays, and turning to the body he said: "Tabitha, arise," [Acts 9: 40], and she opens her eyes and sits up; and he gives her his hand and raises her up, and presents her alive to the saints and the widows. This is made known through all Joppe, and many believe on the Lord.

St. Peter sojourns many days at Joppe, in the house of Simon, a tanner; for there the Lord had wondrous work for him to perform. Whilst he was staying at Joppe, St. Peter, on a certain day, about the sixth hour, goes up onto the higher parts of the house to pray, and whilst they are preparing something for him to eat, he falls into an ecstasy, and he sees heaven opened, and a certain vessel descending, as it were a great sheet let down by the four corners from heaven to earth; in this are all manner of four-footed beasts and creeping things of the earth and fowls of the air, and he hears a voice saying to him: "Arise, Peter, kill and eat;" and Peter, in reply to this, says: "Far be it from me, Lord, for I have never eaten any common and unclean thing:" Again a second time, he hears the same voice speaking to him, and saying: "That which God hath purified, do not thou call common." This was done three times. [Acts 10: 13-16.]

Whilst St. Peter is doubting what this means, and what could be the nature of the vision, certain persons come from Cornelius, a centurion who dwelt at Caesarea – he was a religious man and feared God – in compliance with directions which had been given him in a vision, to request Peter to come with them to Caesarea. St. Peter again hears the Spirit addressing him saying: "Behold, three men seek thee. Arise, therefore; go down, and go with them doubting nothing, for I have sent them." [Acts 10: 20.] St. Peter goes down to them, and they tell him how that Cornelius had received answer of a holy angel to send for him into his house, and to hear words from him. St. Peter lodges them in his house for that night, and on the day following he goes with them, some of those from Joppe accompanying him.

When St. Peter arrives at Caesarea, he meets Cornelius, and goes in with him to his house, and finds many of the friends of Cornelius assembled there; and he tells them that they knew how abominable a thing it was for a man who was a Jew to keep company with any person of other nations; but that God had shown him how he was to call nothing common or unclean; therefore he came when he was sent for. He desires also to know the cause of their sending for him. To this Cornelius replies in the following words: "Four days ago, until this hour, I was praying in my house at the ninth hour, and behold a man stood before me in white apparel, and said: Cornelius, thy prayer is heard, and thy alms are remembered in the sight of God. Send, therefore, to Joppe, and call hither Simon, who is surnamed Peter; he lodgeth in house of one Simon, a tanner, by the sea-side. Immediately, therefore, I sent to thee, and thou hast done well in coming. Now, therefore, all we are present in thy sight, to hear all things whatsoever are commanded thee by the lord." [Acts 10: 30-33.]

St. Peter, in reply to the request made to him by Cornelius and his friends, said to them: "I perceive that God is no respecter of persons; but in every nation he that feareth him, and worketh justice, is acceptable to him." [Acts 10: 34-35.] He then proceeds to tell them how the word of God had been published through all Judea, and how our Lord had gone about doing good, and healing all who were oppressed by the devil, and that he and the other apostles were the witnesses of these things, as they were also of his resurrection. He then declares to them how they were commanded to preach to the people, and to testify that our Lord hath been appointed to be Judge of the living and of the dead.

Whilst St. Peter was yet speaking these words, the Holy Ghost fell upon all them that were hearing the word. This caused much astonishment amongst the members of the Church who had been Jews; for they wondered that the grace of the Holy Ghost was also poured out upon the Gentiles, and that they should hear them speak with tongues and magnify God.

St. Peter then asked them: "Can any man forbid water, that these should not be baptized, who have received the Holy Ghost as well as we?" [Acts 10: 47.] And he then commanded them to be baptized in the name of the Lord Jesus. Thus was the Vicar of Christ deputed to receive the Gentiles within the fold of the Church.

Through the kindness of the Emperor Tiberius, who showed much favor to the Church, the spirit of persecution which had been raised against it ceased, and peace was at length restored to it. The apostles left Jerusalem to spread the doctrines of Christianity; and they commenced with Syria, and with the countries which were situated near Jerusalem and Judea. St. Peter departs from Judea, and proceeds to Syria, the capital of which was Antioch.

St. Jerome, Eusebius, and the ancient writers agree in their statements respecting Antioch being the first episcopal see of St. Peter, and that the apostle governed this city during the space of seven years. The faithful were first called Christians in this city [Acts 11: 26], as St. Gregory the Great also informs us in one of his Epistles. [Lib. vii., Epist. 40.] It was but just that the prince of the apostles should be its first pastor. During the period that St. Peter ruled the see of Antioch, he was constant in making missionary tours into other countries, that he might convert all who desired to become members of the Church. He preached the faith to the Gentiles in the provinces of Pontus, Galatia, Cappadocia, and Bithynia. About the year 37, St. Peter was visited by St. Paul in Jerusalem, who spent fifteen days with him, and acquaints him with his conversion, and acknowledges him to be the supreme head of the Church.

In the divisions which the apostles made of the different places where they proposed to preach the gospel, St. Peter selected the city of Rome, the capital of the world, and the principal theater of his apostolic labors. This city the prince of darkness had caused to become the center of superstition and error. Here wickedness reigned in its basest forms, and superstition exercised its influence by the worship of false gods. Rome had become the center of power and of all earthly authority, being raised to this high position in accordance with the designs of Providence, who had desired that through these means the Church might be propagated, and the gospel spread throughout the world. It was the design of our blessed Lord to plant the rock on which his Church was founded in the metropolis of the world, in order that the faith might be spread with the greater rapidity, and with greater ease, amongst the nations who were subject to the dominion of that city, which was afterwards to be called the Eternal City. The many difficulties which surrounded the great object which the apostle had in view only increased his zeal, and made him anxious to perform greater acts of devotion in behalf of the Church of which he was the supreme head.

A Biography of the First Pope

Chapter III

Denials that St. Peter was ever at Rome Arise

Marsilius' Hostility to Pope John XXII – His Assertion that
St. Peter had Never been at Rome – Testimony Proving that
he had.

St. Peter, having arrived at the capital of the
Roman Empire, and having, as it were, by his presence
taken possession of the city of Rome, was faithful to the
trust which had been committed to him, and with zeal
and diligence preached the gospel to all who were
willing to receive its powerful influences. On his way
there he had planted the faith in different places: at
Pisa, in Sicily, and at Naples. In the latter city he is
said to have consecrated its first bishop, having said
Mass on an altar which was erected on the spot where
afterwards was built the Church of St. Peter and Aram
[Basilica di San Pietro ad Aram].

The year 40, or as some authors affirm, the year
45, is fixed as the date of the arrival of the apostle in the
city of Rome; who also state that on the 18th of January
he established his See there, having translated it from
Antioch. Before the fourteenth century no person,
however hostile he was to the Holy See, had ventured
to deny that St. Peter was Bishop of Rome, and had
dwelt for many years in the city of the Caesars.
Marsilius, of Padua, [d. 1342], was the first person who
advanced such a statement as this.

On the death of Henry VII, Louis Duke of Bavaria claimed the Bavarian crown, to the exclusion of Frederic, the son of Albert I of Austria. The Pontiff John XXII, had espoused the cause of Frederic; because of this, Marsilius of Padua [circa 1275-1342], who was a firm supporter of Louis, offered every indignity to the Holy See. He carried his hostility so far, that the denied all connection between St. Peter and the See of Rome. St. Peter, he said, had never been at Rome, and consequently, John XXII, who claimed supremacy over the Catholic world, as the successor of St. Peter, the first Bishop of Rome, claimed that supremacy without any lawful grounds, and consequently he was not the supreme pontiff. Errors against the plainest facts of history were followed by errors against the faith of the Church, and as the number of whose who departed from the faith increased they adopted the statements of Marsilius.

Wycliffe, and after him Luther, joined in making these false statements. Calvin seems also unwilling to allow the fact of St. Peter's ever having been at Rome, for the extent of his admissions respecting it amount to this: "that there is nothing repugnant in the statement." Since the days of Calvin there have been many writers who have maintained that St. Peter was never at Rome; but the great and learned men of every creed and of every country have ever zealously vindicated the truth of history, and have been zealous in their maintaining the connection of St. Peter with the See of Rome. The result of this has been, that the fact of St. Peter's residence in the Eternal City has been established on a firmer basis than almost any other circumstance connected with the history of that time. [The controversy continues to this day; please see reference in the Introduction.]

Cave [Wm. Cave, d. 1713], Pearson [Jn. Pearson, d. 1686], Whiston [Wm. Whiston, d. 1752], Young, Blondel [D. Blondel, d. 1655], and others, all authors of eminence, and opposed to the supremacy of the Holy See, have written against the system of Marsilius, and have united with the most eminent Catholic writers in showing the fallacies contained in the writings of those who suppose that St. Peter never had been at Rome.

It may prove both interesting, in connection with a life of the apostle, and also instructive, to enter into a consideration of this matter. To do this effectually it will be necessary to divide the subject into distinct heads. In the first place, the testimony of some of the leading writers of the four or five first centuries, who have left us a record of their opinions respecting this matter, will be addressed. In the second place the causes will be assigned which are said to have drawn the great apostle to Rome. Then, in the third place, some facts of a local character will be stated, and which cannot be explained by any other means than by allowing the residence of the apostle in the Eternal City.

Cave, a writer opposed to the supremacy of the Holy See, has well observed, that if there be one fact of history which is affirmed continuously, it is this of St. Peter's residence in the holy city. Should you reject this, the only conclusion you can come to is, that history is a mighty conspiracy against truth, and we must become skeptical with respect to all matters which are recorded in it.

The first testimony which shall be adduced are the words of Eusebius, in which he refers to the statement of Papias, and Clement of Alexandria, both of whom lived in the second century:

"Under the reign of Claudius, by the benign and gracious providence of God, Peter, that powerful and great apostle, who by his courage took the lead of all the rest, was conducted to Rome, against the pest of mankind, [Simon Magus]. He was a noble general of God, armed with heavenly weapons; he brought the precious merchandise of intellectual light from the east to the dwellers in the west, announcing the light itself, and salutary doctrine of the soul, the proclamation of the kingdom of God. The divine word having been thus established among the Romans, the power of Simon [Magus] was soon extinguished and destroyed, together with the man. So greatly, however, did the spirit of piety enlighten the minds of Peter's hearers, that it was not sufficient to hear but once, nor to receive the unwritten doctrine of the gospel of God, but they persevered, in every variety of entreaties, to solicit Mark, as the companion of St. Peter; and whose Gospel we have, that he should leave them a monument of the doctrine thus orally communicated, in writing; nor did they cease their solicitations until they had prevailed with the man; and thus become the means of that history which is called The Gospel according to St. Mark. They say, also, that the apostle Peter, having ascertained what was done, by the revelation of the Spirit, was delighted with the zealous ardor expressed by these men, and that the history obtained his authority for the purpose of being read in the churches. This account is given by Clement, in the sixth book of his Institutions, whose testimony is corroborated by that of Papias, Bishop of Hieropolis." [Eusebius, I, ii, c. 14,15.]

♦♦♦

The Papias here spoken of flourished about the year 118. Probably he was the disciple of the apostle St. John, and the friend of St. Polycarp. What we know of him for certain is this, that he was most diligent in collecting all kinds of facts regarding the apostles, from those who had been intimately acquainted with them. "If," he says, "I meet with any one who had been a follower of the elders anywhere, I made it a point to inquire what were the declarations of the elders, what was said by Andrew, Peter, or Philip, what by Thomas, James, John, Matthew, or any other of the disciples of our Lord; what was said by Aristion, and presbyter John, disciples of the Lord; for I do not think that I derived so much benefit from books as from the living voice of those that are still surviving." [Eusebius, I iii. c. 39.]

This same century supplies us with three other ecclesiastical writers who have referred to the residence of St. Peter at Rome. Caius, who visited Rome during the pontificate of Zephyrinus, thus refers, in his Disputations with Proclus, to the tombs of St. Peter and

St. Paul: "I can show you the trophies of the apostles, for, if you will go to the Vatican, or to the Ostian road, you will find the trophies of those who have laid the foundation of this [the Roman] Church." [Ib. I. ii.c. 25.]

And the illustrious prelate St. Dionysius of Corinth, who became bishop in 170, in his address to the Romans, speaking of the martyrdom of St. Peter and St. Paul, says: "Thus likewise you, by means of this admonition, have mingled the flourishing seed that had been planted by Peter and Paul at Rome and Corinth, for both of these having planted us at Corinth, likewise instructed us; and having in like manner taught in Italy, they suffered martyrdom about the same time." [Ib.]

St. Irenaeus, a more learned writer than any of those hitherto cited, and who was born about the middle of the second century, presents us with the following testimonies connected with this subject: "Matthew produced his Gospel, written among the Hebrews, in their own dialect, whilst Peter and Paul proclaimed the gospel and founded the Church at Rome." [Ib. I. v. c. 3.] He repeats this testimony in his famous work against heresies, in the following terms: "But as it would be a very long task to enumerate in such a volume as this, the successions of all the churches, pointing out the tradition which is the greatest, and most ancient, and universally known Church, founded and constituted at Rome, by the two most glorious apostles Peter and Paul, derives from the apostles, and that faith announced to all men, which, through the succession of [her] bishops, has come down to us. We confound all those who in any way assemble otherwise than as behooveth them." [Here. I. iii. c. 3.]

The establishment of the Church of Rome, through the ministry of St. Peter and St. Paul, is spoken of here again as a fact beyond question. That Church was most universally known; its origin was best investigated and established, and this is the result of the inquiry: St. Peter had been at Rome, and had founded the Church there.

The third century offers us the voluminous writings of the first African ecclesiastical author, Tertullian. Over and over again he refers to St. Peter's founding the Roman Church and dying there.

"Come now, thou who wilt exercise thy curiosity to better purpose, run over the apostolic chairs of the apostles to this very time; preside over their own places in which their own authentic letters are read, echoing the voice and making the face of each present. Is Achaia near, then thou hast Corinth; if thou are not far from Macedonia, thou has Philippi, thou hast the Thessalonians; if thou canst travel into Asia, thou hast Ephesus; but if thou are near Italy, thou hast Rome, whence an authority is ready at hand to us. Oh, how happy is that Church in which the apostles have poured out all their doctrine with their blood, where Peter had a like passion with his Lord, where Paul is crowned with an end like the Baptist, where the Apostle John was plunged into boiling oil!" [De Pros. n. 35,36.]

In other writings beside that from which the above quotation has been made, he refers constantly to the planting of the faith and the death of St. Peter at

Rome. He, like all the other authorities, speaks confidently, his words evidently regarding it as an acknowledged fact; not a thing to be proved, but a matter of public notoriety.

Origen has left us the tradition of former times relative to the countries assigned to each of the apostles for the work of the ministry; speaking of St. Peter he says: "Peter appears to have preached through Pontus, Galatia, Bithynia, Cappadocia, and Asia, to the Jews that were scattered abroad, who also, finally coming to Rome, was crucified, with his head downwards, himself having requested to suffer in that way." [Eusebius, 1, iii. c. 1.]

Lactantius, in his work on the death of his persecutors, and also in his fourth book on the true wisdom, agrees with the preceding writers. In the former work he states: "When Nero reigned, Peter came to Rome, and having wrought some miracles, which he effected by the might of the Almighty power to this effect being given to him by him, he converted many to justice, and raised up to God a faithful and enduring temple. When Nero was informed of this, and he saw that, not only at Rome but everywhere, a great multitude day by day abandoned the worship of idols and passed over to the new religion, to the rejection of the ancient one, being, as he was, an execrable tyrant, he rushed forward to destroy the heavenly temple, and the first of all others persecuting the servants of God, he affixed Peter to a cross and Paul he slew." [Do Morte Persec. c. ii. p. 523.]

Eusebius' sentiments with regard to St. Peter's visit to Rome have already been alluded to. He repeats the same remarks, not once or twice but several times, and in such a manner as to convince the reader that what he states was universally believed to be true.

St. Peter of Alexandria, who was martyred A.D. 311, after he had governed the see of that city for eleven years, speaks of the prince of the apostles in the following terms: "Peter, the ruler of the apostles, after having been often seized and imprisoned, and ignominiously treated, was at length crucified at Rome." [Apud Galland, t. iv., p. 98.]

St. Optatus of Melevis defies even the Donatists, the worst and most daring enemies of the Church, to deny that St. Peter had been at Rome: "Thou canst not, then, deny that thou knowest that the episcopal chair was given, in the city of Rome, to Peter the first of all others, in which Peter, the head of all the apostles sat. . . Peter, therefore, first filled that preeminent chair which is the first mark of the Church. To him succeeded Linus." [De Schis. Don. ii. 2-4.]

St. Jerome, who was well acquainted with the history of the Church of Rome, having resided there for a long period, and acted as secretary to one of the pontiffs, Pope Damasus, thus mentions St. Peter, in his Catalogue of Ecclesiastical Writers: "Simon Peter, the Son of John, of the province of Galilee, from the village of Bethsaida, the brother of Andrew the apostle, and the prince of the apostles, after his episcopate in the Church of Antioch, and his preaching to those scattered about, of the circumcision, who had believed, in Pontus, Galatia, Cappadocia, Asia, and Bithynia, goes to Rome, in the second year of Claudius, to overthrow Simon Magus; and there he held the sacerdotal chair for five-

and-twenty years, down to the last, that is, to the 14th year of Nero. Buried at Rome, in the Vatican, near the triumphal way, he is honored by the veneration of the whole city."

Rufinus, the opponent of St. Jerome, is as clear on this head as any other writer: "Peter," he says, "ruled the Roman Church for twenty-four years." [Invect. In S. Hieron, 2. p. 661.]

St. Augustine constantly appeals to the authority of that chair at Rome in which Peter sat: "Nay," he says, in his work against the Letters of Petilian, "if all throughout the world were such as you most idly slander them what has the chair of the Roman Church, in which St. Peter sat, and in which Anastasius now sits, done to this?" The east knew as well as the west of St. Peter's journey to Rome; the Christians at Antioch pointed with pride to St. Peter as the founder of their see, but they were forced to admit that Antioch could not keep for ever the prince of the apostles as its bishop.

"This," writes St. John Chrysostom, "is one of the privileges of this our city [Antioch], that it had at first as teacher the leader of the apostles. For it was befitting that that city which, before the rest of the world, was crowned with the Christian's name, should receive as shepherd the first of the apostles; but after having had him as our teacher, we did not retain him, but surrendered him to regal Rome." [T. 111, Home 24.] "It [Rome] contains within it," says Theodoret, "the tombs of our common fathers and teachers of the truth, Peter and Paul – tombs which illuminate the souls of the faithful. Their thrice-blessed and divine twin star rose indeed in the east, but had the setting of its existence by choice in the west, and thence even now illuminates the whole world. These have made your throne most illustrious; this is the culminating point to your blessings; and their God has even now made illustrious their throne, having established thereon your Holiness, emitting the rays of orthodoxy." [T. 4, Ep. 113.]

This letter was addressed to Pope Leo. Every expression and allusion obviously regards the unvarying tradition of St. Peter's preaching and dying at Rome.

Pope Innocent's words would seem at first sight nearly a transcript of those of St. Chrysostom which we have just adduced: "Observe," he writes, "that this [privilege] has been assigned to this city [Antioch] not so much on account of its magnificence, as because it is known to have been the first see of the first apostle, where the Christian faith took its name, and thus had the honor to have held within it a most celebrated assembly of the apostles – a city which would not yield to the see of the city of Rome, save that it was honored by him but temporarily, whereas this city [Rome] glories in having received him to herself, and that he here consummated [his martyrdom]." [Ep. 24. n. 1.]

The testimony of another pontiff will draw the first part of the argument to a conclusion.

Pope Gelasius thus clearly and elegantly expresses himself with respect to the prince of the apostles: "There were assuredly twelve apostles, endowed with equal merits and equal dignity, and whereas they all shone equally with spiritual light, yet it was Christ's will that one amongst them should be the chief, and him by an admirable dispensation did he guide to Rome, the queen of nations, that in the principal or first city he might direct that first and principal [apostle] St. Peter." [T. 10, Galland, p. 677.]

♦♦♦

Chapter IV

Arrival at Rome

Simon Magus – He promises to fly to the Heavenly
Abodes – Struck to the earth at the Prayer of St. Peter – His
Death – St. Augustine's Statement.

It has already been stated that one of the causes
of St. Peter's going to Rome is frequently referred to by
the fathers of the Church, and assists much in
elucidating the truth of the events connected with the
residence of St. Peter in Rome, and seems to confirm a
fact which the east and the west, Greece and Italy,
Africa and Gaul, have believed in for more than
eighteen centuries.

According to Eusebius, St. Jerome, and Orosius,
St. Peter visited Rome for the first time in the second
year of Claudius, the emperor, which corresponds with
the forty-second of the Christian era; and he went
thither, if we may believe the statements of Eusebius
and St. Jerome, in order to silence the heresiarch Simon
Magus: "Immediately under the reign of Claudius . . .
Peter, the powerful and great apostle . . . was conducted
to Rome against this pest of mankind." [Galland, 1. ii.
c. 14.]

St. Jerome also bears testimony to the same fact:
"Simon, the son of John . . . the brother of Andrew the
apostle, and the prince of the apostles, goes to Rome, in

the second year of Claudius, to overthrow Simon Magus." [Cat. Scrip. Ecc. 1.]

Of this infamous man Magus, St. Justin makes distinct and detailed mention in his first Apology, addressed to [Emperor] Antoninus Pius. We are told that he was a Samaritan, of the village of Giton, was versed in magic, and was so successful in the practice of his art as to become at first the wonder and glory of the Romans, and eventually the object of their adoration. He informs us farther of the time when this man flourished, the place where his statue was set up, the inscription it bore: "To Simon the holy God;" and he also tells us that his companion was an abandoned person of the name of Helena. He also proceeds to exhort the emperor to communicate these particulars to the Senate and the people, in order "that if any of them should chance to be entangled by the doctrines of Magus, they might at length free themselves from the trammels of error;" and finally he prays "that the statue raised to the impostor might be taken down." [Apol. I. c. 34.]

With equal distinctness Tertullian alludes to the heresiarch, and rebukes the Romans for adoring such a worthless man.

Vincent of Lerins, in his Commonitory, refers to the overthrow of Magus, who has been emphatically called by the fathers, "the parent of heretics:" "Was not Simon Magus the first so deservedly smitten by the apostolic sword? . . . Was not this conjurer, I say, the first who had the face to charge God the Creator as the author of all evil?" [Common, c. 30.]

But there are still more particular statements to be made with respect to St. Peter himself. Arnobius wrote his Apology either at the close of the third or as early as in the fourth century as the year 303. In the second book of this work the following words occur: "The men were engaged by the arts of King Numa, and the ancient superstitions in this city [Rome], still they did not hesitate about abandoning the concerns of their country, and uniting in the admission of Christian truth, for they beheld the car of Simon Magus and his fiery steeds blown away by the truth of Peter, and brought to nothing at the name of Christ."

It appears that even the catechumens were instructed about this event, for St. Cyril of Jerusalem, in his Sixth Catechetical Address, tells them: "The error of Simon spreading farther and farther, the illustrious pair of men, Peter and Paul, the rulers of the Church, corrected it by going thither, who soon exhibited as dead the putative god, on his appearance; for when Simon had declared that he would ascend aloft into heaven, . . . the servants of God . . . cast him headlong on the earth; . . . and though this occurrence was wonderful in itself, it was not wonderful under the circumstances, for it was Peter who did it, he who bears with him the keys of heaven; it is not worth our wonder, for it was Paul who did it, he who was caught up into the third heaven."

◆◆◆

St. Cyril's testimony agrees with those already cited, as to the main facts of the magician's defeat at

Rome by St. Peter. In one respect, however, he differs from the writers already cited, for he supposes this event to have taken place in the reign of Nero, and not in the time of Claudius. Many writers agree with Cyril in placing the downfall of Simon Magus in the reign of Nero.

The legates of the holy see, in a letter to Eusebius of Vercelli, also make mention of this event: "For the Lord and his Christ know that on the arrival of the most blessed apostles, the name of God is glorified in the overthrow of Simon."

St. Pacian plainly refers to this well-known story: Does not Peter confound Simon in the presence of the judge? Does not Paul blind Elymas?" [Epist. ii. Ad Symb.]

Epiphanius, when writing on the heresy of the Simonians, refers to the occurrence in the following words: "Simon, we know, paid the debt of Nature at Rome, when falling he dies miserably in the midst of the city of the Romans." [Heb. xxi. 5.]

St. Ambrose, in the work entitled Egesippus, which he wrote while still young and a catechumen, enters into greater detail: He tells us "that Simon promised to fly, and thus ascend to the heavenly abodes. On the day agreed upon he went to the Capitoline Hill, and, throwing himself from the rock, began his ascent. Then Peter, standing in the midst, said: 'O Lord Jesus, show him that his arts are vain.' Hardly had these words been uttered, when the wings which Simon had made use of became entangled, and he fell. His thigh was fractured, never to be healed; and some time afterwards the unhappy man died at Aretia, where he had retired after his discomfiture."

In another of his works Epiphanius refers to the same fact: "Peter overthrew and laid prostrate Simon, as he soared to heaven by magic flight, by breaking the power of his charms."

Philostrius of Brixia, in his observations on the heresy of Simon, says "that when the heresiarch arrived in Rome where he would contend with the blessed apostle [Peter], in the presence of Nero the king, being completely overthrown by the power of the blessed apostle, and stricken by an angel, he merited such a death as made the evident lie of his magic patent to all men."

St. Augustine, the illustrious prelate of Africa, in several places distinctly alludes to St. Peter's overcoming Simon at Rome. In the beginning of his book on heresies, he says: "In which city [Rome] the apostle Peter overcame him by the true power of the Almighty God."

In answer to all these statements, which are so striking, and which so fully prove St. Peter's being at Rome, it is alleged by writers of an infidel turn of mind, that Simon is a myth, and his doings mere fabulous legends, or mere romances got up to adorn the life of St. Peter. For the following reasons this statement would appear to be devoid of truth. Those writers who have been referred to, as may be seen, speak absolutely about the personality and deeds of the impostor. Even the Apologists, as Justin, Tertullian, and Vincent of Lerins, speak in as plain terms about him as about any other well-known individual; nor could they refer even emperors and a Roman senate to the history of a fictitious person, for by doing this they render their own proceedings of no avail, and they would have materially injured the cause of Christianity. An inaccuracy of this nature would have done an amount of mischief which volumes of truths would not have sufficed to repair.

St. Augustine informs us that as Aeneas was proclaimed a god after his death, by the Latins, so was Sangus likewise by the Sabines, and therefore the inscription which was discovered with "Sangus" on it, refers to him, and is altogether different from the inscription recorded by Justin, and which has already been referred to; therefore the objection drawn from the discovery of this statue, and which the writers before referred to speak so much of, is of no avail, as it does not militate against the statement of Justin, who refers to a different statue and a different inscription altogether.

◆◆◆

Chapter V

Rome as Babylon

St. Peter Dates his First Epistle from Rome – Testimony of
Papias, Valesius, and Grotius, to that Effect.

If further proof be needed of the sojourn of St.
Peter at Rome, the following reasons will supply this.

All critics of any weight or authority assert it, as
a certain rule, that any circumstance which a writer of
respectability, who lived either at the time or near the
time when the event which he records took place, is to
be believed, unless a writer of earlier date or one whose
testimony is more worthy, does not profess to believe in
it.

A public fact which all the faithful, and which
even those who do not hold the faith, have believed to
be true for fifteen centuries, must be supposed to have
taken place, although there would be no other record for
it in existence than the fact of its being believed in for
so long a time.

When men write about public circumstances,
and about matters referring to history, they satisfy
themselves about the truth of these, not only from
books and writings but also from public monuments,
from inscriptions, and from privileges and immunities
conferred on any particular city or state, for all these
have authority in determining whether the matter
referred to took place or not.

The law of nations and public faith require that credit should be given to any city or state recording those things, while those who relate them must have sufficient opportunity of knowing whether they took place or were connected with their public history.

All reasonings or arguments, unless they be direct historical proofs, are of no weight when adduced against a circumstance which is supported by contemporaneous history by unanimous consent, and by a tradition of many ages; and if what has been already stated be called to mind, it will be found that the journey of St. Peter to Rome is to be accounted amongst those facts which the above rules relate to, for as we have seen, it is referred to by Papias, Clement of Alexandria, Origen, Tertullian, and several other writers of the second or third century; and, as we shall see in the following chapters, there are public monuments existing in Rome, connected with St. Peter's stay in that city.

The Roman pontiffs, from the time of SS. Peter and Paul, have maintained the supreme authority in the Church, and all the honors and privileges connected with this high position. The conclusion from all these proofs is evident – that St. Peter's visiting Rome rests upon such historical proofs, that all the arguments of those who profess to disbelieve it cannot call it into question.

But there is another argument remaining to be stated in connection with this subject. This is the testimony of St. Peter himself, who dates his first Epistle from Rome – as all eminent writers interpret this passage in his first Epistle: "The Church which is in

Babylon, elected together, saluteth you." [1 Peter 5: 13.] In calling the city of Rome Babylon, the apostle seems to have been influenced by motives of prudence, that he might not indicate to the many enemies which he had, the place of his residence, and by his doing so, subject himself to constant persecution. This he was ever ready to suffer when it came upon him, but to bring it upon himself needlessly, might well be looked upon as a tempting of Providence. It should also be remembered that he was writing to those of Hebrew origin, who were familiar with figurative language, from perusing the writings of the prophets which abound in this style of speech. It had been usual to call a wicked city, Sodom, a country given to idolatry, Egypt, a people under a curse, Chanaan, a city which was filled with wickedness, and which might be looked upon in the light of an enemy, Babylon. This city had been the place where their ancestors suffered captivity, and it had despoiled their ancestors of their country and of their kingdom. Pagan Rome resembled this in many respects; for it had reduced Judea into a province, and had already persecuted the Christians, and stirred up the hatred of its inhabitants against them.

When St. Peter dwelt at Rome, and when he wrote to the strangers dispersed through Pontus, Galatia, Cappadocia, Asia, and Bithynia, it was natural to call Rome by the name of Babylon, being the name by which these persons, as ancient writers tell us, were accustomed to call that city. Papias informs us, that St. Peter wrote his first Epistle at Rome, and that he referred to Rome, when he made use of these words: "The Church which is in Babylon, elected together, saluteth you." And Valesius, a writer of note, states that those who wish to refer the Babylon spoken of by St. Peter to the eastern metropolis of that name, are going contrary to the opinion of eastern writers; and Grotius, a writer whose belief would have led him to have adopted a different opinion, if facts were not too strong against him, writes as follows: "The new and the old interpreters differed respecting Babylon. The old interpreters refer it to Rome, where no true Christian ever doubted that St. Peter had been; the new ones state that Babylon in Chaldea is meant by it; I however, agree with the old." [Grotius on 1 Peter 5: 13; Hugo Grotius 1583-1645.]

It also appears that the Jews, to whom St. Peter wrote his Epistle, would not be likely to apply Babylon to the city of that name which was in Chaldea, for it appears from the testimony of Pliny, that it was rather a heap of stones than a city. Strabo speaks of it as nearly altogether deserted; Diodorus speaks of it as having only its smallest part inhabited. They also add, that a short time before the reign of Claudius, in the reign of Caius, the Jews were banished from Babylon, and came to Seleucia.

Josephus gives a more detailed account of this event. He says, "that the Babylonians, Anilaus and his companions being put to death, attacked the Jews, who, deeming themselves not equal to enter a contest with them, fled to Seleucia, where they were safe from any assault for fifty years; that six years after this a pestilence raged in the city, and that a few families of the Jews who had not yet migrated from the city, came to Seleucia, where a dreadful calamity overpowered them, for the Greeks and the Syrians, who were the inhabitants of the city, though hitherto they were not on good terms, entered into a league to destroy the Jews, and slew more than fifty thousand of them; and those who escaped from the slaughter went to Neesda and Nesbis, esteeming themselves safer there."

◆◆◆

There was a village in Egypt called Babylon, which is now the modern Cairo. This appears to have been built by the Persians, when Cambyses, who as also king of Egypt, permitted the Persians to settle in that country. In the time of Strabo, one of the Roman legions, which had been emancipated in Egypt, retired there, as into a strong fortification; but there does not appear to have been either Jews or Christians residing there. Nor is it asserted by any eminent writer that St. Peter went there, or preached the gospel there. Nor does it appear to have had a bishop before the time of the Council of Chalcedon, whose name was Cyrus according to Spanheim. Baronius, however, states that the first bishop of this place was called Zosimus, and that in the fifth century, when Justin was emperor, he ruled over the church in that city.

If St. Peter had established a church there, it could not have remained unknown through so many ages; and if he were writing to the Jews of this place, he would have added some word which would have marked it more distinctly, that there might not have been a possibility of confounding it with Babylon of Chaldea – a city which was nearer to them, and being more closely connected with their history, and with the various events which took place during the time they had dwelt in Palestine. Besides, it has never been shown that St. Peter crossed the Euphrates, or ever visited Babylon in Chaldea or Babylon in Egypt. Neither Scripture nor ecclesiastical history even allude to such an event ever having taken place. There is therefore no reason for departing from the usually received interpretation, and for not supposing that St. Peter meant by Babylon the city of Rome.

The Jews to whom St. Peter wrote could not suppose that the apostle alluded either to Babylon in Chaldea or Babylon in Egypt, and, as we have seen, it was more natural that they should believe he referred to pagan Rome, which, as a city filled with iniquity, might well be called Babylon.

The passage in the first Epistle of St. Peter, where he speaks of the church which is in Babylon, could not have remained unknown for so many centuries, as those who are not inclined to admit that the apostle in these words refers to pagan Rome would have us believe. Whoever read the passage would at once come to the conclusion whether Babylon was to be understood in an allegorical sense or in a literal sense. The most illiterate as well as the most learned would soon make up their minds on this point, and having once done so, would not hastily change; they could not be at a very great loss to find out where St. Peter was when he wrote this Epistle, and then they would infer that he was proposing to designate that place by the name of Babylon. We do not find any person doubting that the apostle was at Rome when he wrote this Epistle.

Those who had read the Epistle would also be able to find out whether St. Peter was ever at Babylon or not, and also whether he was at Rome when he wrote the Epistle. It does not appear that any writer mentions any difference of opinion having existed respecting this matter; they all seem to conclude that by Babylon St. Peter intends to designate the city of Rome, then the capital of the pagan world. It would also seem that these persons held this as an apostolic tradition, which had been handed town to them by the apostles themselves, or by their disciples.

Modern writers would oppose this, though they adduce no arguments or authorities of any weight to corroborate their statements. The differences which exist in their interpretations of this passage show also their want of unity, and that they are destitute of that which has ever been looked upon as a mark of truth – agreement in the main facts of the statements which are made. The fathers and the Catholic interpreters have always taught, without any one attempting to deny it, from the first ages of the church until the present day, that St. Peter, in his first Epistle, by Babylon intended to point out Rome, as the place which he wrote this first Epistle. Their statement has met with no contradiction until of late years. The conclusion is evident that it must be looked upon as true.

It has been stated as an objection of St. Peter's being at Rome, that the different writers have not been agreed amongst themselves as to the exact year when he first came there; but this objection is of no weight, for though the writers may differ in their statements respecting the date of the apostle's coming to Rome, they all are unanimous in maintaining the fact of his coming there. Lactanius places the time of St. Peter's coming to Rome in the reign of Nero; Eusebius, St. Jerome and others fix the date in the second year of Claudius. Many of the ancient fathers say that he was Bishop of Rome for twenty-five years. St. Paul, though dwelling at Rome, and having written many Epistles from it, nowhere mentions ever being at the capital of the pagan world. It is also added that Claudius, in the year 49, in the ninth year of his reign, banished all the Jews from Rome, and that therefore St. Peter must have left it at that period.

It may be said in reply to those who maintain that St. Peter was never at Rome, because the writers differ about the year when he came there, that the Church affirms nothing respecting the time when St. Peter came to that city; all that it maintains is, that St. Peter was at Rome; and gives perfect liberty to follow the writer who maintains with the clearest arguments what seems to be the true date. Those who place the advent of St. Peter to Rome in the second year of Claudius, and those who maintain that he came there when that emperor began his reign, do not differ from each other; for when Claudius reigned thirteen years, the second year of this emperor may be called the beginning of his reign.

Though it may be maintained that St. Peter was bishop of Rome for twenty-five years, it is not to be inferred from thence that he remained there during all that time; for, as the necessities of the Church required it, he could go to the east or the west, and yet not have given up his see, as the bishops who, in the present time, are obliged to visit the holy city, are not said to have given up their see, because they go away from it for a short time; and from the second year of Claudius to the last year of Nero a space of exactly twenty-five years intervened. Nor is there any difficulty in reconciling those statements which differ from each other; for it is probable that St. Peter came to Rome, according to the opinion of St. Jerome, Eusebius, and other writers, in the second year of the reign of Claudius, and then left it for some time; but returned again in the 12th or 13th year of the reign of Nero, shortly before he suffered martyrdom; and, being cast into prison, suffered together with St. Paul, in the year 66, on the 29th of June, the day in which the Church celebrates their martyrdom.

Nor is there any thing strange in St. Paul, in writing to others from Rome, or in writing to the Romans his Epistle, not mentioning St. Peter, when St. Peter was absent from Rome at that time. It is stated as a strong objection against the apostle's being at Rome, that it is recorded in the Acts of the Apostles that the Jews dwelling at Rome, whom St. Paul questioned respecting the Christian religion – and told the nature of the persecution he underwent – that they stated the only knowledge they had respecting the Christian religion was that it was spoken against everywhere; for they told him: "For as concerning this sect we know that it is everywhere contradicted." [Acts 28: 22.] It would appear that these Jews were not of the fold of Christ, and, imbued with the false opinions which they had received from the calumnies and writings of the Hebrews, were acquainted with the Christian religion only by name; and when St. Paul came to Rome, they eagerly flocked to hear him.

Knowing that he was a learned man, they were anxious to hear something more respecting the Christians against whom the synagogue had been so greatly excited; and although many of the Jews who dwelt at Rome, as also many of the heathens, had embraced the faith, as they did not frequent the synagogue, there is no difficulty in supposing that the Jews had not heard of the Epistle which St. Paul had written to the Romans; therefore it is natural to expect that they should be unacquainted with the labors both of St. Paul and St Peter, in propagating the faith.

It would appear that when SS. Peter and Paul had resolved to devote themselves, one exclusively to the Jews, and the other to the Gentiles, they did not intend thereby to preclude themselves from preaching to either Gentiles or Jews, whenever an opportunity should present itself. St. Peter administered the sacrament of Baptism to Cornelius and his entire household; and St. Paul, wherever he went, or in whatever city he dwelt, first preached the faith to the Jews and afterwards to the Gentiles, when there seemed to be a hope of converting them to the faith. St. Peter, without neglecting the Gentiles, made it his duty to bring the Jews within the fold of the Church; and St. Paul followed a like course with respect to the Gentiles, always instructing them, yet without declining, whenever an opportunity presented itself, to make the Jews participators in the same blessings.

At Rome St Peter would find an ample field for exercising his mission; for, when Herod died, Josephus informs us that the ambassadors who came from Jerusalem to Rome, to request that they might for the future be free from the government of the kings, brought twelve thousand Jews with them. [Antiqu. t. 17, c. 12.] And Philo records that the part of Rome beyond the Tiber now called Trastevere was chiefly inhabited by the Jews. [Legat ad Caium.] In the reign of Claudius there were so many Jews residing at Rome that he feared a tumult. He did not however dare to expel them from the city, but was content to forbid their assembling together. It appears, however, on account of the Christians, they were constantly engaging in tumultuous proceedings. [Suetonius in Claudio.]

It is very probable that St. Peter left Rome at this time, and returned in the sixth year of Nero, who did not persecute the Jews but only exercised his cruel disposition in persecuting the Christians. Near the conclusion of the reign of Nero, all ancient writers affirm that St. Peter and St. Paul both returned to Rome, where they suffered martyrdom. The objection which is sometimes urged, from no mention being made in the Acts of the Apostles of St. Peter's being at Rome, is not of much force; for St. Luke does not profess to write a history of St. Peter, or to give an account of his life. After the sixteenth chapter of the Acts of the Apostles, he seems altogether to forget St. Peter, in order that he may devote himself to give a lengthened account of the labors of St. Paul.

Spanheim, in order that he might invalidate the testimony which has been adduced to show that St.

Peter was at Rome, has collected an immense number of legends respecting the places which St. Peter visited, also respecting the churches and altars which are said to have been consecrated by him and the bishops of the different cities who were the companions of his journeys. To these he has added many circumstances which bear upon them the stamp of falsehood. But it is clear that these cannot invalidate the truth of the question which he wishes to disprove, that St. Peter was at Rome and lived there for many years, no more than the false statements and foolish stories which the Jews have connected with the life of our Lord and his apostles, would show that such a person never existed, and that he was not crucified in Jerusalem; for the duty of the critic is not to reject the principal facts of history because they may be sometimes colored with false assertions, but to select the true from the false, the certain from the doubtful, and genuine facts from the false adjuncts with which they may be encumbered.

But the labors of our adversaries do not even rest here, they make use of all possible means to weaken the force of the testimony of the writers which have been already adduced. They say that Papias was a credulous and simple-minded man, and believed in every story that he might chance to hear; they affirm that the quotations made from Ignatius are false, and that the Epistle which he wrote from Smyrna to the Romans is incorrectly attributed to him. They add to these assertions that Irenaeus, Clement of Alexandria, Tertullian, and Origen have committed many errors, both respecting time and places, in their writings, and are not therefore worthy of credit. This is however a very poor way to elude the authority of the fathers, and to seek to invalidate their writings. If the fathers and writers of the first three centuries are of no weight, and of no authority respecting matters of fact, what grounds have our adversaries for their opinions, and for the creeds which they profess to hold and to teach? Many of the dogmas of our holy religion are so closely connected with facts, and so interwoven with them, that they cannot be separated from them.

If we reject the testimony of Ignatius, of Clement of Alexandria, of Tertullian, and of the writers of the first three centuries, where can we find other writers whose authority is of greater weight than these? If Origen and Tertullian erred in matters of faith, this will not serve to invalidate their testimony respecting a fact publicly known, and which was of such interest to religion in general, that it could not possibly remain unknown.

The only conclusion we can arrive at respecting this matter is that St. Peter came to Rome and was bishop of that see for twenty-five years, and that one of the principal objects he had in view when he came to that city, was to put an end to the evil machinations of Simon Magus; and that it also appears that the Babylon from which he dates his first epistle is not to be taken as referring to Babylon in Egypt, nor Babylon in Chaldea, but that the apostle intends by this to refer to Rome.

♦♦♦

A Biography of the First Pope

Chapter VI

Suffering and Death of St. Peter

The Chains of St. Peter in the Church of St. Pietro in Vincoli – The Mamertine Prison, the Place of his Confinement – The Ostian Way, where our Lord appeared to St. Peter – Crucifixion of St. Peter.

There are local circumstances connected with St. Peter's dwelling in the Eternal City which will give additional weight to the arguments which have been already stated. In no other part of the world save in Rome shall we find spots pointed out as places hallowed by the imprisonment and crucifixion of the apostle, and also by his tomb; in no other city in the world are there existing monuments which refer to a person who lived eighteen centuries ago [now two millennia], such as those connected with St. Peter in Rome.

The hill on which he suffered is shown, and the spot is now hallowed by having a circular chapel erected over it, which has a dome supported by sixteen Doric columns of black granite, and was built at the expense of Ferdinand IV, the king of Spain; it is near the church of St. Peter in Montorio, the hill called Montorio being considered as part of the Vatican and not as part of the Janiculum. This spot appears to have been selected by Nero that he might be able to witness the martyrdom of the apostle from the palace in which he lived on the Palatine Hill. There St. Peter was crucified with his head downward, as he esteemed it too high an honor to be crucified like his divine Master.

The first Christians who hallowed by lasting monuments, the principal places which were made sacred by the footsteps of the apostles, were careful to mark this spot, which was rendered sacred by the death of St. Peter, and the Church of St. Peter in Montorio has become one of the most beautiful in that part of the city of Rome.

"His chains also are shown, those chains which he wore to give liberty to the world. They may be seen in the Church of St. Pietro in Vincoli, at Rome, any day during the octave of the festival, on the day in Lent on which the station is held there; at other times they are kept in a small silver box, which is placed in a large chest fastened by two locks, one key of which is kept by the abbot of the monastery, and the other by the major domo of the sacred palace, and is never opened without the written order of the pontiff, unless on the station in Lent and during the octave of the festival, when they are exposed on an altar in the church, over which is a painting of the miraculous deliverance of St. Peter from prison.

"Eudosia, the wife of the Emperor Theodosius the Younger, going to Jerusalem, received there the chains with which the apostle was bound by Herod: these chains she afterwards sent to her daughter Eudoxia, to Rome, who gave them to the pope; he showed her another chain with which Nero had bound the same apostle, and when the pontiff placed the chains near each other, they became miraculously united, and form now but one chain; the different structure of the two parts of the chain is clearly marked." [Neligan's Rome, p. 135; see also Appendix II below.]

The place of his imprisonment is also shown.

"The Mamertine prison is situated on the north-eastern extremity of the Capitoline Hill, and is said to have been erected by Ancus Martius. The prison is divided into the upper and lower. The descent into the first is by a modern staircase made when it was converted into a sacred place. The first prison is thirty feet long, twenty-two feet wide, and fourteen feet high; there was a hole in the roof through which the criminals were let down by a cord; under this was a similar hole leading to the lower prison, the descent to which is now by a modern staircase; this lower prison is twenty-two feet long, nine feet wide, and six feet high. An inscription on the wall of the upper prison states it was restored by the consuls Vibrius and Cocceus Nerva, in the year of Rome 574. Although the entrance was towards the capitol, the ascent to it was on the side of the forum, near the commencement of the steps called the

Scala Gemonia. These steps joined the prison by means of a stone bridge; from their summit the bodies of criminals were thrown, in order to terrify the people who were in the forum.

"In this prison Jugurtha died of hunger; the accomplices of Cataline's conspiracy were strangled here; here, also, was put to death Aristobulus and Sejanus after the triumph of Pompey, Sejanus by the order of Tiberius; and Simon, the chief of the Jews, by the order of Titus. As the conquerer ascended to the capitol in triumph, the prisoners were thrown into this lower prison, being brought there by the Scala Gemonia, where they were put to death; when this was accomplished the cry 'autum est' – it is done – told the conqueror he might now leave the temple.

"But other impressions than these fill the Christian as he enters the place. Here St. Peter and St. Paul were both imprisoned; from this place they were taken the day they went to execution. We kissed with respect the column to which they were bound, we drank water from the fountain which St. Peter caused to come forth from the floor, that he might baptize St. Processus and St. Martinianus, their jailers, with the twenty-seven soldiers, who were all martyred in their turn. There are altars in each of these prisons." [Ibid., pp. 79-80.]

The spot is also pointed out where he resided, and the altar on which he offered up the sacrifice of the Mass. These are now within the Church of St. Pudentiana:

"St. Peter having arrived at Rome about the year 44, with the desire of planting the cross on the summit of the capitol, went at first to the part of the city near the Tiber, being the quarter of the Jews. He soon converted the Senator Pudens, his mother Priscilla, and his two sons, Novatius and Timotheus, and his two daughters, Praxedes and Pudentiana, with their servants. The house of this devout neophyte soon became the residence of the apostle. There St. Peter celebrated the august mysteries, and consecrated Linus and Cletus, this was no doubt the title of the Pastor which we so often read of in the early writers; whoever has seen those mosaics in the aisle near the altar, on which St. Peter so often said Mass, must be satisfied as to the antiquity of the place. Here, too, is the well into which these holy virgins squeezed the blood of martyrs which they had collected with sponges; here, too, they hid the bodies of the martyrs and their remains, which they had gathered up. Pius I, in the second century, changed the senatorial house into a church with the title of the Pastor." [Ibid., pp. 69-70.] [Pastore or Pastor was the name of the first owner or presbyter of the house or church.]

"On the Ostian Way is also shown the place where Christ appeared to St. Peter, and which is called, '*Domine quo vadis.*' This church, founded in the early times of the Church, attests a fact which the Catholic pilgrim dwells on with pleasure. St. Peter had been confined in the Mamertine Prison, and was in daily expectation of the sentence being carried into execution which had been passed on him. The Christians, fearful of losing their chief pastor, had resolved to rescue him, and having succeeded in their attempt, the saint was now outside the walls of the city, traveling on the Appian Way, by which he had entered Rome twenty-five years before. When he had arrived at the place where this church is now built, he perceived his Divine Master coming to meet him, bearing his cross. Peter recognizing him, said '*Domine quo vadis.*' Our Lord replied '*Venio iterum crucifigi.*' St. Peter understood him, and returned to Rome, and there awaited the cross on which his Divine Master was about to suffer again, in the person of his vicar. The constant tradition of the faithful at Rome attests the truth of the apparition of our Lord; and St. Ambrose, in his discourse against Auxentius, alludes to it." [Ibid. p. 271].

♦♦♦

Nor are these the only evidences which we have of the residence of the apostle in the holy city. The pictorial catalogue of the popes, as well as the mural and other inscriptions, all testify to the same fact. This everlasting pointing to the history of St. Peter, this inability to separate the city and the apostles, give us additional proof, if it be needed, of the residence of the apostle in the holy city. No other city claims the honors which Rome monopolizes, of having St. Peter, the prince of the apostles, as its first bishop. [Although St. Peter founded the church at Antioch, the official catalog of its bishops lists Evodius as the first; see online Catholic Encyclopedia article "The Church of Antioch," at newadvent.org.] The world knows, and it has always known, that Rome was the city signally favored by God and St. Peter, and that there is no possibility of opposing the prescription which Rome can urge in its favor. "We must remember, writes one who seems to have examined these matters with impartiality, "that St. Peter was crucified on this hill, but was buried at the Vatican." I should be inclined to believe the latter tradition, and perhaps the former may also be true; but the place of interment is more likely to have been kept in remembrance that that of his suffering. Even some Catholic writers have differed as to the precise spot where he was crucified. Eusebius appeals to a constant tradition that St. Peter was buried in a cemetery at the Vatican, and quotes the authority of Caius, who lived in the early part of the third century. [On June 26, 1968, Pope Paul VI announced that the bones of St. Peter had been discovered in a necropolis underneath St. Peter's Basilica at the Vatican, although some archeologists dispute the finding.]

"Some writers have thought it necessary to deny that St. Peter was ever at Rome. I confess I am utterly at a loss to see what great advantage is given to Catholics by allowing their first pope to have resided at Rome. But, at all events, truth is to be preferred to prejudice . . . . After examining the evidence produced by Baronius, the conclusion seems irresistible, that St. Peter undoubtedly visited Rome, and suffered martyrdom there. The only question is concerning the period of his residence. It used to be maintained that he held the see of Rome for twenty-five years . . . The only ancient authors that can be quoted as asserting it, are Eusebius and Jerome . . . We read in the Chronicle of Eusebius, in the year 43, that Peter, after founding the Church at Antioch, was sent to Rome, where he preached the gospel for twenty-five years, and was bishop of that city." [Burton, H. E. b. ii., c. 25.]

Such was the language of one [Protestant] who looks upon the fact of St. Peter's being at Rome as indisputable; for the evidence which established it is too plain to be avoided or rejected. The rejection would involve, as this writer insinuates, the rejection of all authentic history; as to the difficulty on which he seems to dwell, it has already been shown to be of no avail; for no Catholic writer ever pretended that St. Peter remained at Rome during the period of twenty-five years, without leaving it, although he had established his episcopal see there.

All suppose he did not remain there; and if they allow that he was the bishop for upwards of twenty-five years, notwithstanding he was absent during many years, they maintain it on precisely the same grounds as they ascribe twenty-three years of spiritual sovereignty to Pius VI, and also to Pius VII, though each of these popes was, for a considerable time, in exile in a foreign land, far away from the city whence they derived the title of Roman Pontiff.

Dollinger, in his work called *The Beginnings of Christianity*, explains the difficulties connected with the chronology in the following manner:

"Following," he says, "the unanimous tradition of Christian antiquity, the apostle Peter was crucified at Rome, after having governed the Church there, in quality of bishop, and transmitted to his successors, with the Roman episcopate, the primacy which Christ had conferred upon him. As to the time of his arrival at Rome, and the duration of his episcopate in that city, opinions are very diverging, as it is impossible to reconcile the date of the ancients on this point otherwise than by admitting that the prince of the apostles was twice in the capital of the world.

"His first abode would fall, according to Eusebius, St. Jerome, and Orosius, in the second year of the reign of Claudius, the forty-second of the Christian era, an epoch in which St. Peter would have gone to have stopped the seductions of Simon the Magician, and would there have established the foundations of a church.

"Then, being included in the edict of banishment which Claudius had promulgated against the Jews, he must quickly have left the capital of the world for Jerusalem, where he was overtaken by the persecution of Agrippa. It would seem that he afterwards undertook a more extensive apostolic journey to Asia Minor, and founded, or visited, the churches of Pontus, Galatia, Cappadocia, and Bithynia, to which he addressed later his evangelical letter from Rome. St. Jerome, however, assigns this excursion into Asia Minor to a period anterior to the apostle's first visit to Rome, somewhat later than St. Peter went to Antioch, and thence to the synod of Jerusalem. Under the reign of Nero he went to Rome for the second time, where he suffered with Paul, in the year 66, the death of a martyr. It is of this journey that Lactantius speaks. Thus may be explained the twenty-five years of episcopacy which are assigned by St. Jerome and Eusebius. There is an interval of twenty-five years from the second year of Claudius to the last year of Nero's reign. As for a continuous residence of twenty-five years duration at Rome, that was never mentioned by any person whatever." [Vol. I., p. 70.]

◆◆◆

One more argument in confirmation of what has already been advanced remains yet to be stated. This argument proceeds on the authority of those fathers of the Church who uniformly assert that St. Mark was the interpreter of St. Peter, and that he wrote at Rome what he heard St. Peter say, in his addresses to the converted Jews in that city. On this point very clear evidence can be adduced. Clement of Alexandria has delivered to us the following tradition, as derived from the oldest proselytes. He says, "that the Gospel of St. Mark was occasioned in the following manner: when Peter had proclaimed the word publicly at Rome, and declared the gospel under the influence of the Spirit, as there was a great number present, they requested Mark, who had followed him from afar, and remembered well what he had said, to reduce these things to writing; and, after composing the Gospel, he gave it to those who requested it of him." [Eusebius, I. vi., c. 14.]

Papias tells us that what he records, he had received from the friends of the apostles, and he makes the following statement, on the authority of John the presbyter: "Mark, being the interpreter of Peter, whatsoever he recorded he wrote with great accuracy, but not, however, in the order in which it was spoken or done by our Lord; for he neither heard nor followed our Lord, but, as before said, he was in company with Peter, who gave him such instruction as was necessary." [Ibid., I. iii., c. 39.]

"Mark," says St. Jerome, "the disciple and interpreter of Peter, at the solicitation of the brethren at Rome, wrote a short gospel, according to what he had heard Peter state, which, when Peter had heard, he approved, and delivered to the church to be read by his authority, as Clement writes in the 6th book of the Hypotyposes; and Papias, the Bishop of Hieropolis, makes mention of this Mark, as Peter does also, in his first Epistle, where Rome is designated figuratively by the name of Babylon: The church which is in Babylon . . . saluteth you, and so doth my son Mark." [De Scrip. Ecc., p. 281.]

Eusebius writes as follows on this subject:

"The divine word having thus been established among the Romans, the power of Simon was soon extinguished and destroyed, together with the man. So greatly, however, did the splendor of piety enlighten the mind of St. Peter's hearers, that it was not sufficient to hear but once, or receive the unwritten doctrine of the Gospel of God, but they persevered in every variety of entreaties to solicit Mark, as the companion of Peter, and whose Gospel we have, that he should leave them a monument of the doctrine, thus orally communicated, in writing. Nor did they cease their solicitations until they had prevailed with the man, and thus become the means of that history which is called the Gospel according to St. Mark. They say, also, that St. Peter having ascertained what was done, by the revelation of the Spirit, was delighted with the zealous ardor expressed by these men and that the history obtained his authority, for the purpose of being read in the churches.

"This account is given by Clement, in the 6th book of his Institutions, whose testimony is corroborated by that of Papias, Bishop of Hieropolis; but Peter makes mention of Mark in the first Epistle, which he is also said to have composed at the same city of Rome, and that he shows this fact by calling the city by an unusual trope, Babylon; thus, "The church at Babylon, elected together with you, saluteth you, as doth also my son Marcus." [Eusebius, I. ii. c. 15.]

The evidence already adduced respecting St. Peter's residence at Rome, is such that no unprejudiced person can any longer doubt the fact. It has been shown that Papias, Clement, Caius, Dionysius of Corinth, Irenaeus, Tertullian, Origen, Lactantius, Eusebius, and Peter of Alexandria, Cyril of Jerusalem, Epiphanius, Ambrose, Jerome, Rufinus, Austin [St. Augustine], Optatus of Melvis, Egysippus, Theodoret, Ambius, Orosius, Innocent, Gelasius, Philastrius of Brixia, all bear testimony to this fact, that Peter visited Rome; or, to state the argument in other words, the representatives of the illustrious churches of Rome, Alexandria, Jerusalem, Corinth, Antioch, and Milan, of Italy, Gaul, Africa, Phrygia, Palestine, and Spain, all testify openly and unhesitatingly, to the fact of Peter's residence in the Eternal City; not one of them speaks doubtingly, not one refers to it as a mere report, not one makes use of language which could lead us to imagine that a doubt had ever been whispered in his hearing opposed to this statement; the testimony is unequivocal, nor is there a writer of antiquity who says one word in maintenance of an opposite opinion; all who refer to the see of Peter, and to the place of his death, speak of Rome as the apostolic see and city of his martyrdom. Whilst silence on this head would not have militated against the fact, the positive testimony already adduced must be admitted as decisive of the question; add to this chain of patristic evidence the local facts which have already been mentioned, and in consequence of which Rome became, from the earliest ages, the resort of pilgrims of every grade and from every quarter of the world, and the fact can no longer be doubted, that St. Peter was at Rome, and bishop of that see for twenty-five years, and suffered martyrdom there, A.D. 66, being crucified with head downwards. Some writers affirm that he was then eighty-six years old.

◆◆◆

Chapter VII

Rock of the Church

Succession of the Popes – St. Peter the Chief of the Apostles – Martyrdom of SS. Peter and Paul.

Note: This last chapter is present in my 1892 copy of this book on St. Peter by Fr. De Ligny. But it refers to an event that occurred after the 1789 death of that author. This final chapter appears to have been edited or updated by Rev. W. Waterworth, S.J., since a variation of it comprises the second chapter of his book *England and Rome,* published in 1854.

◆◆◆

That St. Peter was bishop of Rome has been clearly proved from the writings of Irenaeus, Tertullian, Optatus, Jerome, Rufinus, Chrysostom, Theodoret, and Innocent. Not only do these writers state that St. Peter was at Rome, but they likewise inform us that he founded and governed the Church in that city; Eusebius and St. Jerome affirm that he governed it during the space of twenty-five years. The See of Rome has been known in ancient as well as in modern times as the see of Peter, and has been called so under the titles "of the see of Peter, Peter's chair, the holy, the apostolic see."

These are the ordinary words by which it is designated now, so also was it wont to be called in olden times. Rome, as St. Cyprian expresses it, is the chair of Peter, and to this chair, all like St. Jerome had recourse in trouble. Although Antioch had been ruled by Peter for seven years, it was not in after ages called the see of Peter; though Jerusalem and other cities could boast of sees established by apostles and apostolic men, not one of these was called continuously the holy see, the apostolical see. These terms and those of like import are applied to Rome, and to Rome exclusively.

The fathers and other ecclesiastical writers have left us catalogues of the popes of the see of Rome. The lists of the principal sees were kept with the greatest care, and to them all members of the Church appealed when establishing their own claims, or when they wished to disprove the claims of heresy to apostolicity. Look at our records, they were wont to say; see how we can ascend from prelate to prelate until we arrive at either an apostle or one directly sent by an apostle; show your lists that prove your Church to be apostolical, and since the Roman Church was, of all others the most illustrious, the most honored, and the best known, and the Church with which all were in communion, hence it happened that to it more frequent appeals were made than to any other church.

At the head of the list of its bishops the name of Peter is always distinctly placed, as appears from the catalogues which are furnished by Eusebius and by Epiphanius. "Linus," writes Eusebius, "whom he (Paul) has mentioned in his 2nd Epistle to Timothy, as his companion at Rome, has been shown to have been the first after Peter who obtained the episcopate at Rome . . . In the second year of Titus's reign, Linus, bishop of this Church, is proved by Paul to have been a fellow-laborer and fellow-soldier with him . . . After Evaristus had completed the eighth year as Pope of Rome, he was succeeded in the episcopal office by Alexander, fifth in succession from Peter and Paul." [Eusebius, I. 3, c. 4.]

Epiphanius's list is more complete than this: "The succession of the Popes of Rome was in the following order: Peter and Paul, Cletus, Clement, Evaristus, Alexander, Xystus, Telesphorus, Hyginus, Pius, Anicetus – the same named by me above as in the list, and let no one wonder that we have gone through each of those matters, for by means of these the manifest truth is pointed out." [Eph. adv. Hev. t. i. p. 107.] St. Augustine writes: "How much more securely and and beneficially do we reckon from Peter himself, to whom, bearing the figure of the Church, the Lord says, 'upon this rock I will build my Church, and the gates of hell shall not overcome it." [St. Aug. t. viii. c. 269.] St. Optatus makes use of nearly the same language as St. Augustine, and says Peter filled the preeminent chair, which is the first mark (of the Church); to him succeeded Linus, to Linus succeeded Clement, to Clement, Anaclete . . . "You who assign to yourselves the holy chair," he adds, writing to the Donatists, "tell us the origin of your chair."

St. Jerome states, in his work on ecclesiastical writers: "Clement, of whom the apostle Paul, writing to the Philippians, says: 'With Clement, and with others my fellow laborers, whose names are written in the book of life,' was the fourth bishop of Rome after St.

Peter, for the second was Linus, the third Anaclete, although many Latins think that Clement was the second after the apostle Peter." [P. 285.]

[The list of the first twelve popes with their dates is now considered to be: St. Peter (32-67), St. Linus (67-76), St. Anacletus (Cletus) (76-88), St. Clement I (88-97), St. Evaristus (97-105), St. Alexander I (105-115), St. Sixtus I (115-125) also called Xystus I, St. Telesphorus (125-136), St. Hyginus (136-140), St. Pius I (140-155), St. Anicetus (155-166), and St. Soter (166-175); please see www.newadvent.org/cathen/12272b.htm.]

◆◆◆

From the ancient catalogues and pictorial representations we have another very powerful argument not only of St. Peter's being Pope of Rome, but also of his being pope there for the space of twenty-five years. The most ancient catalogue we have on record was drawn up about the year 354, during the pontificate of Liberius. To St. Peter it assigns twenty-five years of episcopacy in Rome; and of all succeeding pontiffs named therein, with the exception of Liberius, the exact term of possession of the Roman see is distinctly recorded. If it be asked why the term of Liberius's episcopacy is not given, it can be said in reply, that he was alive when that list was drawn up. This presents us with an authority anterior to the catalogue of St. Jerome, and yet agreeing completely with it.

Since the fourth century numerous catalogues have been drawn up, some of greater and some of lesser antiquity, but in all these St. Peter ever stands forth as the first Pontiff of Rome, and, furthermore, the long term of twenty-five years is assigned to his episcopacy; he is the head, the leader, the founder, of the pontifical succession at Rome. Him the popes of all nations look upon as the first of the Roman line. It matters not who occupies the apostolic chair, or to what nation he belongs, the statement which he makes is this, that he is a successor of St. Peter. This fact can be only explained in one way – by acknowledging that the whole world was aware and convinced of the fact of St. Peter having been bishop of imperial Rome.

To give the catalogue in detail of the Roman pontiffs, would not seem necessary in a brief sketch like the present, as it may be found in a very interesting and learned work published a few years ago by the Benedictines of Solesmes [*Origines de l'Eglise Romaine*]. In this work the reader will find the antiquity of each catalogue learnedly and clearly established. There is, however, one catalogue to which it may be interesting to make some allusion.

In the famous Basilica of St. Paul Outside the Walls, on the Ostian Way, which was destroyed by fire on the 15th of July, 1823, but which has now been rebuilt with a degree of magnificence which rivals its ancient splendor, is to be seen a pictorial list of the pontiffs, together with a duration of each pontiff's government. This list was begun as early, at least, as the time of Leo the Great (A.D. 440) or, as others will have it, as early as 423, and to it additions had constantly been made down to the present time. This catalogue of the popes, like the others, begins with St. Peter, and the following memorial was affixed to his likeness: "Petrus sed. ann. 25, m. 2, d. 27." Peter sat (in this see) 25 years, 2 months, and 27 days.

From all that has been said the conclusion is plain, that St. Peter was not only bishop at Rome, but that he was also bishop of Rome for a lengthened period, and also that the fact is better supported than the histories of the Caesars, the Assueruses, the Herods, and the Etheldreds who have ruled nations. Let any one endeavor to fix the chronology of the reigns of these sovereigns, and he will soon find that the evidences which he will be able to adduce in favor of his system will not be half so respectable, or so ancient, or so abundant, as that which has been adduced in proof of St. Peter's journey to Rome, and living there as bishop of the Eternal City.

The conclusion which follows from the fact of St. Peter being bishop of Rome is important, and one which every Catholic looks upon as the foundation of his faith; for if St. Peter was bishop of Rome he was also head of the entire Church, the ruler of the spiritual kingdom of God, and the shepherd of a mighty flock. To the truth of this, Scripture and history alike bear evidence. To one possessed of faith it appears clear that there is hardly one truth – certainly that one truth would not be either the mystery of the Holy Trinity or the Divinity of God the Son, who became incarnate for our sakes – more clearly referred to, and indeed expressed, in Holy Writ, than the supremacy of St. Peter.

As Bossuet well observes:

"Peter appears the first in every way, the first in making profession of faith, the first in the obligation of exercising charity, the first of all the apostles who saw our Saviour risen from the dead, as he was also the first to witness before the people, the first when there was question of filling up the number of the apostles, the first to confirm the faith by a miracle, the first to convert the Jews, the first to receive the Gentiles, the first everywhere; but it is impossible to say all. Every thing concurs in establishing his primacy. Yes, every thing even his faults . . . The power given to several is not bestowed without restriction, whilst that given to one alone, and over all, and without exception, is communicated in full. . . All receive the same power, but not in the same degree, nor to the same extent.

"Jesus Christ begins with the first, and in this first he develops all the rest . . . in order to teach us that ecclesiastical authority, first established in the person of one, has only been disseminated on condition of being always recalled to its principle of unity, and that all those who shall have to exercise it ought to hold themselves inseparably united to the same chair: it is that chair so celebrated by the fathers of the Church, in exalting which they have vied with one another, attributing to it the principality of the apostolic chair, the chief principality, the source of unity, the highest degree of sacerdotal dignity, the mother church, which holds in her hand the conduct of all other churches, the head of the episcopate whence proceeds the light of government, the principal chair, the only chair, through which alone all are able to preserve unity.

"In these words you hear St. Optatus, St. Augustine, St. Cyprian, St. Irenaeus, St. Prosper, St. Aritis, St. Theodoret, the Council of Chalcedon, and the other councils, Africa, Gaul, Greece, Asia, the East, and the West, united together . . . Since it was the design of God to permit that there should arise heresies and schisms, there was no constitution that could sustain itself more firmly or more powerfully bear them down. By this constitution every thing in the church is strong, because every thing therein is divine and united, and as each part is divine, the bond also is divine, and all together is such, that each part acts with the power of the whole." [Bossuet, Sermon sur l'Unitė, part i.]

♦♦♦

But for the Catholic reader there is no need to dwell on this point, for he knows that if this supremacy be destroyed, the source of unity and jurisdiction is gone, and the Church of the world is rent asunder; establish it and the world is Catholic.

Well may the fathers apply the following titles to St. Peter: "the solid rock," "the great foundation," "to him the keys of the kingdom were granted," "to him the sheep were assigned, and he is the universal shepherd," "he is he pillar of the Church, the buttress, and the principal, and the source of unity," "he is the eye of the apostles," "the mouth of the apostles," "the tongue of the apostles," "the head of the apostles," "the highest of the apostles," "the corypheus [conductor] of the choir of the apostles," "the prince of the apostles," "a leader of his own brethren," "the one chosen out of the twelve," "the one preferred before all," "the only one who has the primacy of the apostleship, and the primacy over the universal Church," "he is set over the whole habitable globe," "he is the fisherman of the universe," "he represents the whole Church," "in fine, he has received the sovereignty."

Such is the language which the fathers have applied to the prince of the apostles. Language like this cannot be equivocal; for it is the language of the eastern and western churches, respecting the supremacy of St. Peter and his being the vicar of Christ on earth.

Already has the death of St. Peter been spoken of, and the manner of it described; something shall now be said about the death of St. Paul:

"St. Peter and St. Paul were shut up in the Mamertine Prison, in the month of October, A. D. 65, and were both taken out on the 29th of June, 66; they passed through the gate Trigemina, when the lictors separated them, according to the orders which they had received. St. Peter was brought to the Vatican, where he was crucified, and St. Paul commenced his journey to the Salvian Waters, where he was beheaded. It is in the church dedicated to St. Paul where he was martyred. [San Paolo alle Tre Fontane - Church of St. Paul of Three Fountains.] In the church are three springs of water, which miraculously gushed forth from the earth where the head of the apostle touched it. In an angle is the column to which the apostle was bound when he was beheaded. Near it is the altar of the saint, ornamented with columns of black porphyry. As the apostle was led to the place where he was martyred, he converted three of the soldiers of the escort, who were martyred three days afterward. As his head was cut off, instead of blood flowing from the body a stream of milk issued from it, which covered the ground and the lictor; the head made three bounds, and three fountains sprung up where it touched the earth, each still preserving a different temperature.

After the execution, Plautilla covered the head of the apostle in her veil, and buried it in a catacomb of Lucina on the Ostian Way, and his body was, by careful attention of Lucina, afterwards conveyed to the same spot. At the same moment the priest Marcellus was giving a royal sepulture to St. Peter, who had been crucified on the heights of the Vatican.

On the spot where the apostles separated before their execution, there is erected a small chapel, with an inscription alluding to this circumstance. Dionysius, in his Epistle to Timothy, speaks of this separation of the apostles, and also of the words they addressed to each other. Paul said to Peter: "Peace be with thee, foundation of the Church and pastor of the lambs of Christ;" and Peter said to Paul: "Go in peace, preacher of the good and guide of the salvation of the just." [Neligan's Rome, pp. 265-269].

◆◆◆

A Biography of the First Pope

Appendix I

Did St. Paul withstand St. Peter to his Face?

[From an Internet article by the editor of this book, Frank Rega, at http://divinefiat.blogspot.com/2015/07/did-st-paul-withstand-st-peter-to-his.html.]

There is ample evidence to suggest that he did not - that the person St. Paul rebuked in this Biblical incident was not Simon Peter, but another "Cephas."

It is an almost universal assumption in today's Catholic world that St. Paul did in fact rebuke the first Pope to his face. As is written in Galatians 2:11: "But when Cephas was come to Antioch, I withstood him to the face, because he was to be blamed." This assumption is used to justify the concept that it is acceptable in extreme circumstances to publicly confront a Pope with what one believes to be his errors, and it is also an argument used to justify "resisting" the ordinances of a Pope.

However, while reading a short but well-documented biography of St. Peter by Fr. François De Ligny SJ, which I came across in an 1892 collection of Catholic writings, the following paragraph immediately struck me:

"That the Cephas who was reprehended by St. Paul for the inconsistency of his conduct with respect to the Mosaic rites, was not St. Peter, is the opinion of the best writers. Eusebius quotes Clement Alexandrinus as maintaining that this Cephas was one of the seventy disciples. This opinion is followed by the most learned writers of antiquity, by St. Jerome, by St. Gregory the Great, by St. Anselm, and by many others." [See page 2 of this book.]

This surprising statement caused me to investigate this issue further.

James Likoudis wrote a two-part article in the late 1990's entitled "Were the Apostle Peter and Cephas of Antioch the same person?" [http://credo.stormloader.com/Doctrine/cephas.htm.] He admits that some of the greatest Fathers and Doctors of the Church, and contemporary exegetes contend that the person confronted by Paul was Simon Peter. However, he then presents arguments published by Jesuit Fr. D. Pujol over a century ago ". . . effectively demonstrating that the Apostle Peter and the Cephas of Antioch and Corinth could not have been the same person." Fr. Pujol asserted that "Whether the dispute at Antioch between Paul and Cephas occurred before or after the Council of Jerusalem, it was chronologically impossible that Peter could have been there at either time.

Likoudis also mentions a vision by the stigmatist Theresa Neuman (d. 1962) in which she revealed:

"Cephas of the Epistle to the Galatians, whom Paul withstood to his face was not Peter, the prince of the Apostles. That there is no mention of this important personage in antiquity is based on the fact that Cephas was drowned in the sea while on a mission tour and thereupon the opinion arose that he did nothing in his new field of endeavor or even fell away from the faith."

Likoudis summarizes the work of other scholars on this issue, and concludes "That Peter and the Cephas (of Antioch and Corinth) are two different personages needs to be seriously re-examined and not be testily dismissed as a 'cockeyed theory'." He further states: "The upshot of all the above is that in Gal. 2:7-14 where Petros is mentioned and then followed by a shift to Cephas, two distinct personages are differentiated."

A quite intriguing article by James M. Scott [https://strawdog.files.wordpress.com/2008/08/cephas.pdf] delves into a 1708 work in Latin by French Jesuit Fr. Jean Hardouin called Dissertatio: In Qua Cepham a Paulo Reprehensum Petrum Non Esse Ostenditur (An Examination in Which It Is Demonstrated that Cephas Rebuked by Paul is not Peter).

The following quotes are representative of the views of Fr. Hardouin:

"Hardouin opens in AD 49, the year of the Jerusalem Council of Acts 15. The general line of this argument is that the Cephas in Antioch in Gal. 2 cannot be Peter, since for chronological and motivational reasons Peter could not have returned to Jerusalem for the Council."

"Hardouin maintains that it is all but impossible that Peter, who never had seen Antioch within the 14 year period from Paul's conversion, would in the fifteenth year "have raced in unbelievable speed" ("incredibili celeritate advolasse") from Jerusalem to Antioch, been rebuked there by Paul, and within a month have hastened back to Jerusalem to be consulted by Paul about the very controversy back in Antioch."

"Hardouin says that Peter must be "clean from any blemish of heresy" ("immunem haereos labe . . . Petrum") and that it is unthinkable that any "Summus Pontifex" would withdraw himself from baptized Christians solely because they were not circumcised."

◆◆◆

For a thorough scriptural analysis of this controversy, I recommend this article [http://oraclesoffire.blogspot.com/2011/08/galatians-2-and-petercephas-controversy.html] by Bryan Davis. Although it is in the interest of Protestants to contend that Peter/Cephas are one and the same, since it implies fallibility, weakness and even sin to Peter, Mr. Davis, who is not Catholic concludes with:

"The evidence, both biblical and historical, is overwhelming that the man Paul confronted in Galatians is not the apostle Peter. That man was named Cephas, likely a Jew who sympathized with the Judaizers . . . Because of Peter's faithful defense of the Gentiles and their reception of the true gospel at every turn, it is important to make sure we do not denigrate Peter's legacy with the false charge that he dissembled in Galatians chapter two. After the Holy Spirit indwelt him at Pentecost, he was sure and steadfast. Let us honor the truth about Peter and clear his name in the church, especially among those who have so greatly benefited from his faithful stand for our inclusion in the faith."

Personally I am convinced that St. Paul did not rebuke St. Peter. Of course this observation is certainly not going to resolve the problem, and scholars, pundits and writers will continue to debate the issue. However, it is clear that there is sufficient room to doubt the conventional scenario that St. Paul withstood St. Peter to his face. Catholics who take comfort in this incident in order to justify a public reproof of a pope or resist his teaching should take heed.

A Biography of the First Pope

Appendix II

St. Peter's Chains
by Father Francis Xavier Weninger (1876)

The Holy Church on August 1 celebrates a special feast in commemoration of the great benefit which God bestowed upon His people by miraculously delivering St. Peter, the visible head of the church, from prison. The entire event is described in the Acts of the Apostles [Chapter 12], by St. Luke. Herod Agrippa, a son of Aristobulus, favored by the Roman Emperor Claudius, ruled over Judaea, with the title of king. To give more stability to his reign, he endeavored to make himself beloved by the Jews, for which there was no easier way than to persecute the Christians, especially those who fearlessly proclaimed the Gospel of Christ, as did the holy Apostles. He had, therefore, apprehended, and soon after beheaded, James the Great, brother of St. John, which bloody deed gave the Jews great satisfaction. To increase this, Herod commanded them to seize St. Peter, intending to make away with him in the same manner. His command was executed; Peter was taken prisoner, chained and locked in a narrow dungeon, which was guarded so vigilantly, that he could not escape. It was then near the Easter

Festival, after which St. Peter was to be beheaded. The Christians, in deep distress, were praying day and night, that the Almighty would not permit His flock to be so soon deprived of its shepherd.

There was no human power to save him; but God, hearing the prayer of His people, delivered him by a miracle. On the eve of the day on which he was to be executed, God sent an Angel to set him free. Although heavily laden with chains, the holy Apostle slept peacefully, guarded by the soldiers. The Angel, who by his brightness, illumined the dungeon, struck him on the side and awakened him, saying: "Arise quickly. Gird thyself; put on thy sandals and cloak and follow me." The Apostle, whose chains had fallen from his hands, and who thought it all a dream, obeyed and followed the Angel. They passed the first and second watches without attracting their attention, and reached the iron gate which led into the street. The gate opened without the aid of human hands. After having conducted St. Peter through one street, the Angel vanished and was seen no more. Not until then did the holy Apostle realize that his deliverance was not a dream but a reality. Hence he began to praise the Almighty, exclaiming: "Now I know truly that the Lord has sent his Angel and delivered me out of the hands of Herod, and from all the expectation of the people of Judaea." He proceeded immediately to the house of Mary, the mother of John Mark, where the faithful were assembled in prayer.

When he knocked at the door, a servant, named Rhode, came, and asked who was there. Judging by the voice that it was Peter, she was so greatly startled with joy and astonishment, that, without opening the door, she ran back to announce the news. They all believed that she was insane, but as she reiterated her words, some said that it must be his guardian Angel. Meanwhile, the Saint repeated his knocking at the door. They opened it and perceived, with amazement, their beloved shepherd safe and free from chains. Their joy on beholding him was as great as had been their grief when he was taken prisoner. Having given the sign for silence, St. Peter related all that had happened to him. They all gave thanks to Divine Providence when he had ended, and learned to trust in future to the heavenly power and mercy.

Among the sermons of St. Chrysostom, there is one in which he asserts, that the chains by which St. Peter had been bound to the ground, came into the possession of the Christians soon after his deliverance, and were held by them in great honor. Eudosia, wife of the emperor Theodosius the Younger, received them as a present from the patriarch Juvenal, when on a visit to the holy places, and sent one of them to the Church at Constantinople. The other she gave to her daughter Eudoxia, who married the Emperor Valentinian III. Eudoxia showed the chain to Pope Sixtus III, who, on his part, showed her the one with which St. Peter had been bound, before the Emperor Nero sentenced him to die. No sooner had the two chains been held together, than they suddenly united as if they had been but one chain and forged by the same hand. This miracle increased the veneration in which these chains were held, and actuated Eudoxia to build a special church at Rome for their keeping, where they can still be seen.

Many sick were healed by their touch and many possessed were delivered; among the latter was a Count of the court of the Emperor Otho, who, in the year 969, was sent to Rome to be freed from the Evil Spirit. Pope John XIII had hardly touched the count's neck with the holy chains, when he was relieved and his torments were ended.

St. Gregory the Great, writes that it was considered a great happiness to possess a few particles filed off from these chains, and that many persons devoutly wore them enclosed in golden crosses and lockets around their necks. Experience has shown that the touch of these crosses or lockets has restored health to many a sick person. A nobleman, who scoffed at this, and, in derision, dared to break one of these crosses, was severely chastised. He was instantly possessed by the Evil One and became so enraged that he took his own life, as St. Gregory relates. St. Augustine states that the iron of these precious chains is justly esteemed far above gold. Blessed are those fetters which touched the apostle and made him a martyr. "The touch of the blessed limbs of St. Peter has sanctified the instruments of torture." In another place the same Saint says: "If the shadow of St. Peter possessed a healing virtue, how much greater power must the chains of his sufferings have derived from him."

Practical Considerations

St. Peter was innocent, yet persecuted, imprisoned, chained and sentenced to die, which shows that God allows His most faithful servants and best friends to be unjustly persecuted. St. Peter was not much disturbed at his imprisonment, but placing his trust in God, he peacefully slept in his chains. May this instruct you how to conduct yourself under trials. A good conscience and submission to the Divine Will were the means by which St. Peter's sleep, even in a dungeon, was not disturbed. Submit also, under all circumstances, to the Divine Will; endeavor to keep your conscience clear; and your mind will, at all times, be cheerful and quiet. As no human assistance was left to St. Peter and he was to be executed the next day, God delivered him by a miracle. Such is frequently the way of the Almighty with us. He waits until danger has reached its height, and we must despair of human help; then He suddenly manifests His power and His mercy. Hence, never give way to despondency in grief or sorrow, but trust in God. "If it has reached its height, hope most; for it is then that God shows most clearly His might," says St. Chrysostom.

A Biography of the First Pope

About the Editor

The author, Frank M. Rega OSF, is a Third Order
Franciscan and the author of many books and articles
on Catholic saints and mystics. His web page is
www.frankrega.com
and his email address is
regaf@aya.yale.edu.

45164757R00058

Made in the USA
Lexington, KY
18 September 2015